The Soviet Union
and Iranian Azerbaijan

To Gustav,
With friendship,
David

About the Book and Author

Iranian Azerbaijan--an ideological battle-field between Moscow and Tehran--has been a target for Soviet takeover since the formation of the USSR. The effort gained impetus when the Red Army occupied northern Iran in 1941, bringing with it a special detachment of Soviet Azeri Communist Party activists whose goal was to stimulate a national liberation movement among their perceived co-nationals in Iran. Their success, reflected in the formation of the Azerbaijan Democratic Republic in 1945, was short-lived; after the de-parture of the Red Army in 1946, the government fell to the Iranian army and many of its promi-nent figures fled across the border to the Azer-baijan SSR.

In the postwar period, a number of institu-tions aimed at directing and coordinating a national liberation movement among the Azeris of Iran sprang up, becoming especially active after the fall of the Shah. Analyzing the development of these institutions in Soviet Azerbaijan and their impact in Iran, Dr. Nissman utilizes rich and unexplored academic, mass media, and propa-ganda sources in the USSR and Iran. He also surveys the development of the political relation-ship between the Azeris of the Soviet Union and those of Iran--who originated the spread of Bol-shevism among Iranian Azeri oil workers in 1905--and examines the legacy of this movement today.

David B. Nissman is a consultant on Soviet Turkic affairs to several U.S. government agencies.

The Soviet Union and Iranian Azerbaijan

The Use of Nationalism for Political Penetration

David B. Nissman

Westview Press / Boulder and London

Westview Special Studies on the Soviet Union and Eastern Europe

Copyright © 1987 by Westview Press, Inc.

Published in 1987 in the United States of America by Westview Press, Inc.;
Frederick A. Praeger, Publisher; 5500 Central Avenue, Boulder, Colorado
80301

Library of Congress Catalog Card Number: 87-50470
ISBN: 0-8133-7318-2

Composition for this book was provided by the author.
This book was produced without formal editing by the publisher.

Printed and bound in the United States of America

The paper used in this publication meets the requirements
of the American National Standard for Permanence of Paper
for Printed Library Materials Z39.48-1984.

6   5   4   3   2   1

Contents

viii

Acknowledgments

An earlier version of this study was prepared for the Department of State as part of its external research program. Views or conclusions expressed herein are solely those of the author and should not be interpreted as representing the official opinion or policy of the Department of State.

I wish to express my sincere thanks to Dr. Paul Goble of the Department of State for providing invaluable assistance and advice throughout the writing of this work, and the late Alvin Kapusta, also of the Department of State, without whose support and friendship this work could not have been completed.

David B. Nissman

1

Introduction

Persia ceded roughly half of what is considered Azerbaijan today to Russia in 1828. Cross-border contacts between the Azeri Turks, who constitute Azerbaijan's core population, continued without interruption for almost a century. The Bolshevik victory in Russia in 1917 and the subsequent Soviet takeover in Baku in 1920 had the effect of breaking off these contacts; the major result of this was that the Azeris of the Soviet Union and their co-nationals in Iran have developed along two entirely different political and social systems for most of this century. In 1941 when the Red Army occupied northern Iran, including Iranian Azerbaijan, Moscow considered the Soviet Azeri political intelligentsia to be politically reliable enough to be used to lay the groundworks for their Southern compatriots' Marxist-Leninist future. Since the Azeri language is essentially the same on both sides of the border, Soviet Azeris were able to act as instruments in communicating the Soviet line, a role which they played very effectively then as now. The present study is basically an examination of the use by the Soviets of the national factor in manipulating political developments in Iran in the Soviet interest; hence, it is more about the Soviet Union, its tactics and propaganda, than about Iran.

The political aspirations nurtured by the Bolsheviks and their Soviet successors for

Iranian Azerbaijan are perhaps the least studied
aspect of the relations between the USSR and
Iran. This gap in our knowledge is a result of
the fact that cross-border relations between
Soviet nationalities and their ethnolinguistic
counterparts linked to them geographically but
separate politically have only recently come to
be considered of strategic, tactical and polit-
itical significance. Thus, there is no body of
literature which treats this matter either generally or specifically, either in Western or
Soviet sources. It must be added that this
applies not only to the Azeris of the Soviet
Union and those of Iran, but also to the Soviet
Turkmens and their counterparts in Iran and
Afghanistan, the Uzbeks of the Uzbek SSR and the
Uzbeks of Afghanistan, the Uighurs of Kazakhstan
SSR and the Uighurs of Sinkiang and others. The
primary political factor which has made the
relationship between Soviet nationalities and
their perceived co-nationals across the border so
important in recent years is the growing Soviet
ideological and propagandistic emphasis on
national liberation.

Of all Soviet-backed national liberation
movements, that concerned with the national
liberation of the Azeris of Iran is the oldest
and the most significant: the 12 million Azeri
Turks, the largest national minority in Iran,
have been consistently exposed to Soviet propaganda for many years. The core of the Iranian
Azeri population is in northwestern Iran, geographically contiguous with the Azerbaijan SSR
and its population of some 6 million Azeri Turks.
They share the same language, a continuity of
culture and tradition and, to a great extent,
history. A Soviet-sponsored national liberation
movement during the Red Army's occupation of
northern Iran (1941-1946) led to the establishment of the Azerbaijan Democratic Republic under
the leadership of the Marxist-Leninist Azerbaijan
Democratic Party in 1945 (although it should be
noted the current Soviet Azeri hagiographical
works stress that the formation of this republic
was a result of a hard-fought national-liberation
struggle which began in 1941). In 1946, shortly
after the Red Army's withdrawal from Iranian

territory, Iranian Azerbaijan reverted to Iranian control, and prominent members and supporters of the Azerbaijan Democratic Party took refuge across the border in Soviet Azerbaijan.

The contemporary Soviet approach to Iranian Azerbaijan draws heavily on their experience there during the Second World War. In Soviet thinking, the period from 1946 to the present has been marked by the national oppression of the Azeris of Iran, the only remedy for which is a renewed national liberation struggle. Since 1955 the study and management of this movement has been orchestrated from Baku.

Moscow has considered Iran to be extremely vulnerable to Soviet pressure since the fall of the Shah. It is a multinational state in which national minorities had been deprived of all aspects of national rights, including the right to use there own languages, for most of the twentieth century. A Soviet success in controlling or manipulating Iran's minorities -- Azeris, Kurds, Baluch and Arabs -- will open the way for control over Iran's rich natural resources and the Soviet advance to the Persian Gulf.

Moscow was not surprised by the fall of the Shah, and state propaganda organs such as Radio Baku and the Azerbaijan Society for Friendship and Cultural Relations with Foreign Countries were well prepared to exploit the potentially revolutionary situation developing in Iran. Their primary efforts were directed at influencing the course of development in Iranian Azerbaijan by establishing dialogues with 'progressive' Iranian Azeri intelligentsia and cultural personalities: the purpose of these dialogues was, and is to emphasize the ethnolinguistic differences between Azeris and the other peoples of Iran and to promote the concept of Azeri autonomy. Accompanying and supporting these emphases were highlights of Azeri achievements under Soviet rule in order to prove the efficacy of the Soviet approach to the nationalities question. As this campaign evolved in the early 1980s, it became clear that Soviet analysts had failed to predict the appeal of Khomeini's policy of a return to Islamic values among the populace as a whole. As

a consequence, overtly Soviet-backed factions
within Iran found themselves isolated from
mainstream politics.

Until the early 1980s the Soviet objective
for the Azeris of Iran was the establishment of
some kind of national and cultural autonomy which
would not divorce them completely from the central government in Tehran. In 1981, however,
Soviet tacticians shifted the stress from a
basically Azeri cultural autonomy in the Iranian
context to a call for 'One Azerbaijan': the idea
of an inevitable unification of Soviet and
Iranian Azerbaijan in the 'near future' to form
one nation-state. The Khomeini government's
response to this was to gradually close down all
'progressive' Azeri-language media on Iranian
language territory, despite guarantees embedded
in the new Constitution of the Islamic Republic
of Iran that Azeri would be recognized as a
'regional' language and that the publication of
media in this language would no longer be forbidden as it had been under the Pahlavis. This
move made it difficult for Soviet planners to
receive feedback from their overtures to the
Iranian Azeri political, literary and cultural
community. A side effect to the 'One Azerbaijan'
slogan was that under its influence Soviet Azeri
writers were able to express a kind of nationalism which, if expressed in a purely Soviet
context, would meet official censure.

The Soviet propaganda campaign has had a
significant effect on post-Shahist Iranian Azeri
thinking. It united 'progressives' and nationalists in a single Azeri cause; national awareness was stimulated to its highest level since
the 1940s. At the same time, many pro-Soviet
factions had been forced underground or into
exile by 1983. An Iranian counterattack designed
to revive Islam in the Soviet Muslim border
republics began to have a perceptible effect. It
is clear that both Iranian Azerbaijan and Soviet
Azerbaijan have been turned into ideological
battlefields in what is essentially a war between
communism and religion.

Primary emphasis in the Soviet approach has
been on the continuity of tradition, especially
'progressive' traditions shared by the Azeri

Turks both north and south of the Araz River.
This has involved a basic reconstruction and
reinterpretation of the Azeri past, highlighting
common origins through the application of lin-
guistics and ethnology -- a scientific field
known as ethnogenetics -- and stressing political
and historical factors which have both unified
and separated them as a people. An understanding
of the contemporary Soviet manipulation of this
mixture of historical reality and Soviet myth is
central to an understanding of the Soviet
approach and its longterm objectives.

The sources employed in this study are
virtually all Soviet, mostly from the Azerbaijan
SSR. Western historiography has never examined
many of the events and movements which played a
role in the evolution of the present situation:
these include the movement of Sheykh Khiyabani in
1920, the role of the Soviet Azeris in the
founding of the Azerbaijan Democratic Republic in
1945 and the Soviet use of Soviet nationalities
in cross-border relations with their ethnolinguistic counterparts in Iran and Afghanistan.
The most critical question of all, namely whether
Soviet and Iranian Azerbaijan can even be considered a single nation outside of a Marxist-
Leninist context has never seriously been
analyzed. Soviet scholarship, in fact, has only
just begun to touch on these matters; as a Soviet
historian recently remarked: "This question has
never received official scientific recognition,
neither in Western nor Soviet historiography"(1).

The lack of studies does not mean there is a
paucity of sources, although they are of a dis-
parate nature: Russian consular reports from the
late XIXth and early XXth centuries reveal the
extent of the cross-border contacts between the
Azeris of the North and the South; the formation
and activities of the Bolshevik organizations in
Iran and the Caucasus is rather well documented
in Soviet sources; the Soviet adventure which
resulted in the establishment of the Soviet Gilan
Republic has been the subject of a major mono-
graph(2) and a number of Soviet post-mortems from
the 1920s; Iranian Azerbaijan under Soviet
occupation and the rise and fall of the
Azerbaijan Democratic Republic have been the

subject of numerous memoirs written by those who
participated in it; the postwar period, especially from 1979 to the present has been and is
the subject of constant discussion in the pages
of the Soviet Azeri media. Above all, the
literature of "longing", i.e., the longing of the
Soviet Azeris for their perceived conationals in
Iran is a dominant school of literature in the
Azerbaijan SSR(3).

The work is organized in a chronological
manner so that events and developments which bear
on the present situation are described in their
proper place in history; it is hoped that this
arrangement will aid readers who may not be
specialists on Azerbaijan, the Soviet Union or
Iran.

NOTES

1. R. A. Seidov, "O natsional'nom
formirovanii Azerbaydzhantsev v Irane", Voprosy
natsional'no-osvoboditel'nogo dvizheniya na
Blizhnem i Srednem Vostoka. (Baku, 1985), p. 36.
2. Schapour Ravasani. Sowjetrepublik Gilan:
Die sozialistische Bewegung im Iran seit Ende des
19.Jhdt. bis 1922. (Berlin, n.d.).
3. David Nissman, "The Origin and
Development of the Literature of 'Longing' in
Azerbaijan". Journal of Turkish Studies,
VIII/1984, pp.199-207.

2

The Bolshevist Movement in Soviet and Iranian Azerbaijan from 1905–1921

Introduction
According to the 1979 Soviet census, the Azeri population totaled 5,477,000, the over-whelming majority of whom dwell in the Azerbaijan SSR or adjoining regions in other republics of the Caucasus. In Iran, the lack of any official census data since 1956 forces one to rely on estimates which vary considerably, depending on the sources employed. A recent Soviet estimate put their numbers in the two ostans provinces) of northwestern Iran at 5.8 million, with an unknown number of Azeris scattered throughout the rest of the country, primarily in Tehran, Kazvin, Hamadan and other urban centers(1). An Iranian Azeri scholar claims that there are some 14-15 million turcophones in Iran, the majority of whom are Azeris(2). It is safe to assume that there are approximately two Azeris in Iran for every one in the Soviet Union.

The historical background of the modern Soviet contention that the Azeris of Iran and the Soviet Union are one people and one nation is based on the generally accepted scholarly inter-pretation of the dating and impact of the waves of successive migrations into the area they presently occupy. During the later period of Pahlavi rule Iranian historians have attempted to systematically repudiate these Soviet claims on ideological and anti-Soviet grounds; these argu-ments were revived once again under the Khomeini regime and persist to the present. An under-

standing of the actual origins of the Azeri
Turkic people is essential in following the
developments in the Soviet interest in Iranian
Azerbaijan as they have evolved since 1917.

Turkic tribes began to spread into the
Caucasus from the north as the result of the
expansion of two steppe confederacies, the Turgut
and Khazar, in the VIIth century. As a consequence of this expansion Turkic Oghuz and
Kipchak tribal units were forced into the North
Caucasus, Arran, Shirvan and Caucasian Albania,
the latter three of which constitute most of the
territory of modern Soviet Azerbaijan. Undergoing
a gradual conversion to Islam, these tribes began
to move to the south and southwest. The first
Muslim dynasty directly traceable to the ante-
cedents of the modern Azerbaijanis, the Sajids,
ruled in western Iranian Azerbaijan and northern
Iraq from 889-929. During this period, the Turks
began to interact ethnically and linguistically
with other peoples, primarily Iranian and
Caucasian, who occupied the same region.

While these early Turkic migrations began to
leave an ethnolinguistic imprint on the region,
it was not until the late Xth century that it
took on its present ethnolinguistic character.
Seljuk invaders (Oghuz Muslim Turks) who had
penetrated as far as Armenia in the late Xth
century occupied northwestern Iran and much of
the Caucasus; in 1054 the qutba (the Muslim
affirmation of secular dominion) was read in the
name of the Seljuk ruler in both Ganja (now
Kirovabad, AzSSR) and Tabriz. From this point
onward the Oghuz ethnic element began to pre-
dominate over the Iranian and other ethnoses in
the region. This was not, however, a one-sided
process: the Seljukate had begun to use Persian
as the language of the court; the Turkic language
was used among the commoners.

The final wave of Turkic in-migration
occurred from the late XIth-early XIIIth centuries, the late Khwarezmian period. During this
time Turkic elements coming primarily from the
Aral Sea and Syr Darya areas of Central Asia
established new settlements throughout the southern Caucasus, Iran, Afghanistan and Anatolia; it
has been suggested that the number of new ar-

rivals totalled some 1,500,000. Subsequent population shifts and changes are explained by a combination of natural growth rates and the turkification of non-Turkic ethnoses which had been in the area prior to the Oghuz Turkic expansion(3).

Modern Azerbaijani is descended from the Oghuz group of languages brought in by the Seljuks. It is most closely related to modern Turkish and, to a lesser extent, Turkmen. Western and Soviet turkologists are in agreement of this classification(4). The contemporary language of Soviet and Iran Azerbaijan differ from each other in the sense that words have been added to or expelled from Soviet Azeri as a result of language reform and language standardization efforts made in the Azerbaijan SSR after 1920, processes which never took place in Iranian Azerbaijan. An additional factor in Iran is that Azeri was banned as an official tool of communication throughout most of the Pahlavi period. Even the name of the language differs: in the Azerbaijan SSR it is called "Azerbayjan dili" and in Iran "turk", "turk dili" or "azeri".

Despite these changes in the Soviet Azeri literary language, the Azeri used both north and south of the border is essentially identical. The Azeris in Iran, however, still use an arabopersian script; in the Azerbaijan SSR a modified Cyrillic alphabet has been used since 1940 -- the arabopersian script was dropped in favor of a Latin alphabet in 1923.

Current Soviet Perceptions of the Azerbaijani Ethnogenesis

In the Soviet Union it is understood implicitly that language is the primary determinant of nationality. Soviet ethnic, linguistic, cultural and historical perceptions are also strongly flavored by the ethnogenetic approach; i.e., the analysis of the evolution of a single people or nation in order to isolate those characteristics which distinguish them from other peoples as well as determining those elements held in common with other peoples or nations. With regard to the Azeris, these discussions are deeply intertwined with the origin of the Turks themselves.

Since the XIXth century, turkologists have
posited a Central Asian or Siberian "Turkic
homeland"; this rather solid hypothesis is based
on the existence of a series of Turkic inscrip-
tions found at the junction of the Orkhon and
Selenga Rivers in Outer Mongolia dating from the
Vth-VIth centuries. Called the Orkhon inscrip-
tions, they contain the earliest known samples of
a Turkic language in the form of an historical
chronicle. As for the period prior to these, all
data on the Turks is protohistorical and highly
speculative. It is their speculative nature which
makes such "data" vulnerable to contemporary
political manipulation.

In the Azerbaijan SSR there has been a
recent effort to establish a Middle Eastern and
Caucasian origin for the Turks, and to assert
that the Azeri language was formed prior to the
Seljuk invasion. In a newspaper account of a
seminar on "problems of the history of the Azerbaijani language" held in Baku in the Spring of
1984, one speaker claimed in an attack on the
classical hypothesis on the Central Asian origin
of the Turkic peoples that "remnants of this
mistaken theory are impeding the study of the
deep strata of the long history of the Azerbaijani language...There is no reason to wonder
at the possibility that the Turkic language
ethnoses such as the Maittans, Khurrites, Az and
other peoples migrated to Central Asia and the
Altay from the Near East and the Transcaucasus"(5). A report on the same seminar which
appeared in the prestigious academic journal
Sovetskaya Tyurkologiya made no reference to a
"mistaken theory" but did note a discussion on
Turko-Sumerian parallels(6).

Claims such as those noted above have a much
greater political relevance than philological. At
present, Azerbaijan is a place, not a people; the
assertion that the precursors to the Azeri Turks
were originally from the Transcaucasus and Near
East serves to strengthen a Soviet claim to the
land of Azerbaijan, including that part situated
in Iran. It is one of the arguments used to refute
Persian historians who maintain that the people
called "Azerbaijanis" are actually Iranian peoples
forcibly turkified during the Mongol invasions(7).

The toponym "Azerbaijan" means "land of
fires" and refers to the perpetual flames (a
consequence of the substantial oil deposits)
which intrigued Greek and Arab geographers since
ancient times. There is, however, some dispute
about where ancient Azerbaijan was located.
Medieval Arabic geographers placed it in Iranian
Azerbaijan. Lands north of the Araz River (which
defines much of the border between Soviet and
Iranian Azerbaijan) were called Arran, Shirvan
and Albania, a point constantly stressed by
Persian historians in their denial of any Soviet
claim to the region. To counter this, a Soviet
Azeri scholar has stressed that

> facts show that from the IIIrd century
> onward, the name Azerbaijan was understood
> at first administratively and later geo-
> graphically to refer to both parts;
> especially in sources dating from the XVIIth
> century Azerbaijan was accepted in its
> unique geographical meaning without dis-
> tinguishing whether it was north or south of
> the Araz River. In the ethnic sense, after a
> certain period the concept 'Azerbaijanis'
> meant one people speaking the same
> language.(8)

One consequence of this nomenclature debate
is that Iranian Azerbaijan is always referred to
as "Southern Azerbaijan" is Soviet Azeri writings
on the subject, and it has also been proposed
that this apply to Russian discussions of the
subject also(9).

Soviet commentators maintain that a unique
Azeri national identity only began to manifest
itself after the establishment of Soviet power in
Baku in 1920, and that the lack of development of
a similar national consciousness in Iranian
Azerbaijan was due to the suppression of Azeri
national culture, including language, under the
Pahlavis. This "national oppression" has been
exploited extensively in Soviet propaganda
directed southward since the end of the Second
World War.

Iranian Perceptions of the Azerbaijani
Ethnogenesis
      In Khomeini's Iran, religious identity is
more meaningful than national identity. Shi'ism,
the state religion, makes no distinction between
a believer's linguistic identity or ethnic origin.
All are equal under Shi'ism. Reinforcing the down-
grading of nationality in Iran is the fact that
Persian has been the primary medium of cultural
expression for centuries. The presence of a substantial Azerbaijani literary tradition dating
from the XIVth century in Iran is considered to be
a result of the Mongol invasions which resulted in
the forcible turkification of a number of Iranian
peoples. A prominent American Iranist concluded
that "turkification did not create 'Azerbajanis',
that is, it did not impart a distinct national
consciousness to the turkified peoples based on
ethnic rivalries, linguistic differences...or the
setting apart of this group on its own territory."(10) From a Soviet point of view, the flaw in
this argument is one of omission: as noted above,
the weight of historical arguments emphasizes
that the turkification process was actually a byproduct of substantial Turkic in-migrations into
Iran lasting over several centuries.
      In a Soviet attack on the treatment of the
Azerbaijan question in Iranian media, an Iranian
journalist is quoted as saying (probably in
regard to the Soviet occupation of Iranian
Azerbaijan in 1941):

      The reason that Iranian Azerbaijan was
      invaded by outsiders was the Turk language.
      After inventing a history and a literature
      for Azerbaijan, they created a new nation.
      With this, they wanted Azerbaijan to
      separate from Iran.(11)

While one might quibble over the journalist's
language, his analysis of the Soviet objective is
not totally inaccurate. In response to this
Iranian contention, a Soviet Azeri wrote that

      a people can only be said to be free when
      they attain national independence. They have
      to be able to read and write in the mother

tongue. Language is the key to history and culture.(12)

After the withdrawal of the Red Army from Iranian territory in 1946, the official use of the Azeri language in Iran was banned once again. In the first days after the Shah left Iran in 1979, numerous Azeri publications -- newspapers, magazines and books -- were published in Tabriz and Tehran. The new Constitution of the Islamic Republic of Iran permitted the use of Azeri as a semi-official "regional" language. Close examination of the content of this media, however, revealed a strong pro-Soviet slant in many of the Iranian Azeri writings. The Khomeini regime, no doubt suspecting Soviet interference in Iran's affairs, closed down all but one of these publications by the end of 1983. The Soviet-Iranian polemics of the post-1979 period concerning these issues will be discussed in detail in later chapters.

The Division of Azerbaijan and Its Consequences

Contemporary Soviet propaganda makes much of the dividing of Azerbaijan into two parts as a result of the Treaty of Turkmanchay in 1828. Thus, it is of significance to examine the real consequences of this treaty.

In the early XIXth century Russia and Persia waged two campaigns against each other, both to Persia's territorial disadvantage. The first campaign was concluded by the Treaty of Gulistan(1813), under the conditions of which Persia ceded Derbent, Baku, Shirvan, Shaki, Karabagh and part of Talysh to Russia, and abandoned her claims to Georgia, Daghestan, Mingrelia, Imeritia and Abkhazia. Certain territories were only vaguely demarcated, primary of which was that land between Yerevan and Lake Gokcha. When Russia occupied Gokcha in 1825, hostilities between the two countries were renewed. By 1827, however, the Russian army was able to occupy both Tabriz and Yerevan. Persia, under Fath Ali Shah, sued for peace. Peace negotiations began in November, 1827 and were concluded in February, 1828 with the Treaty of Turkmanchay, the border agreements of which remain in force to this day.

In Article Three of this treaty Persia ceded all claims to the Khanates of Yerevan and Nakhchyvan to the Empire of Russia; Article Four delineated the border between the two countries as the Araz River east to the 48th parallel, then dipped south to include part of the Talysh, then moved eastward to the Caspian. In addition, Russian citizens received extraterritorial privileges in Persia, privileges which were later extended to other Europeans. In essence, this meant that Persia had ceased to be an independent country(13).

An official Soviet history of Azerbaijan states that as a result of the Treaty of Turkmanchay, "the one Azerbaijani people was divided in two by force. From that time onward, the historical development of Southern and Northern Azerbaijan began to take different roads"(14). In fact, nothing could be further from the truth.

The establishment of Russian power in the Transcaucasus coupled with the development of Russian capitalism strengthened the economic relationship between the northwestern provinces of Iran - Azerbaijan and Gilan - and Russian Azerbaijan(15). With the industrialization of Baku, a consequence of the exploitation of the Caspian oil fields, a Muslim urban proletariat began to take shape; included in its number were thousands of unskilled and semi-skilled workers from Iranian Azerbaijan. Between 1880-1890 some 30,000 Iranians a year applied for and received visas in order to take employment in the oil fields and factories near Baku, and it has been estimated that if one took into consideration those entering Russia without passes, this number would be closer to 100,000(16). The former Russian consul in Tabriz noted that between 30,000-60,000 passes were issued a year in Tabriz between 1891-1904(17). As a result of this in-migration into Russian Azerbaijan, 50 percent of all Muslim workers in Baku were from Iran during the last years of the XIXth century and the first years of the XXth(18).

The rise of capitalism in the region was accompanied by the development and proliferation of the Azerbaijani press and educational reforms

directed at broadening the base of popular
education among Muslims. Movements advocating
various types of political and religious reform
also began to emerge. Under these circumstances,
it is hardly surprising that the Muslim working
force of Baku had become a target for political
agitation by the turn of the century.

Bolshevik and Marxist-Leninist Organizations in Azerbaijan

A merchant and capitalistic class emerged
among the Azeris at the same time as the proletariat. As pointed out by an official Soviet
history of Azerbaijan, "the Azeri bourgeoisie was
closely connected with Tsarism, which it considered to be the defender of its own interests"(19). One consequence of this relationship
is that the children of this new class were
exposed to the ideas of social justice and new
political directions which had been imported from
St. Petersburg, Istanbul and Paris; at the same
time, many of them had had the opportunity to
study in westernized schools, such as the Gori
Seminary, a division of which had been established for the Muslim elite. Reform was also
occurring in some of the more traditional
madrasas, in which courses in the physical
sciences, history and languages such as French
were added to the traditional curriculum of
exegeses of the Koran, Arabic and Persian
beginning in the 1880s. Nonetheless, the literacy
rate among the Muslims in Azerbaijan remained
extremely low. While the ideas of social democracy and Marxism began to spread among the Muslim proletariat of Baku in the earlier XXth
century, it must be added that initially these
were disseminated by an extremely small number of
Muslim intelligentsia, and committed membership
in the newly emerging political parties was also
extremely small.

Soviet sources claim that the establishment
of a Bolshevik presence in Iranian Azerbaijan
began among the Muslim workers of Baku. The
Russian Social Democratic Workers Party(RSDWP)
had been active in Baku since before the turn of
the century, but had been unable, or unwilling to
attract the Muslim workers to its cause. In 1904,

however, a small group of Azeri intelligentsia
formed a political study group called Hummat
(Endeavor), which engaged itself in discussions
of the various ideas of social democracy which
were surfacing in Europe and Russia. After the
1905 Russian revolution, Hummat merged with the
RSDWP, but retained its autonomy(20). Under
Hummat's auspices, Iranian workers in Baku were
organized into a party named the Ijtimaiyyun-
Amiyyun in 1906; the Iranians were primarily from
Iranian Azerbaijan. The Ijtimaiyyun-Amiyyun was
initially headed by Nariman Narimanov, a prominent Azeri Bolshevik who was to become a con-
fidant of Lenin and the dominant figure in Azeri
politics after the Bolshevik takeover in
1920(21). This has led one Soviet historian to
claim that "Iranian social democracy was founded
with the help and direct participation of the
Bolsheviks of the Transcaucasus"(22).

Narimanov was not the only Bolshevik to hone
his organizational skills on the Iranian workers
of Baku; in 1919-1920 the Bolshevik journalist
and political organizer Seyid Jafar Javadzade,
subse-quently known primarily under the name
Pishevari, served on the Central Committee of the
Adalat Party, which had succeeded the
Ijtimaiyyun-Amiyyun in 1916. In 1920 he was one
of the architects of Adalat's merger into the
Communist Party of Iran(CPI). In 1921 he played a
major role in the Gilan Soviet Republic, and in
1945-1946 served as Prime Minister of the Azerbaijan Democratic Republic. Iranian Azerbaijan
was perhaps one of the most important training
grounds for Azeri communist organizers(23).

The role of the Imperial Russian Army was
also significant in the politicization of Iranian
Azerbaijan. It maintained a garrison in Tabriz
until 1918, where some of its members had formed
Soviets of Soldiers Deputies which attempted to
exert an influence on other social democratic
organizations which had emerged in Iranian Azerbaijan. One of their primary targets was Sheykh
Mohammed Khiyabani, who headed the Azerbaijan
Provincial Committee of the non-Marxist Iran
Democratic Party. Due to their successes in
recruiting local members, the Soviet of Soldiers
Deputies changed its name to the Tabriz Soviet of

Soldiers and Citizens Deputies in the hope of
gaining broader public support. Soviet historians
now claim that Sheykh Khiyabani "supported a
relationship with the Bolsheviks of the Transcaucasus"(24) through the Tabriz Soviet. If this
was the case, the relationship was not a
reciprocal one(see below).

The Establishment of Soviet Azerbaijan
One result of the turmoil in Russia ensuing
from the February Revolution(1917) was that the
Caucasian provinces -- Armenia, Georgia and
Azerbaijan -- were able to break away and form
their own independent states. In Azerbaijan in
1918 the government was formed under the leadership of the Musavat Party (officially called
the Turkish Federalist Musavat Party) which was
basically centrist and nationalist in orientation. This period of independence was short-
lived for both external and internal reasons: the
formation of a Soviet government in Russia and
the British occupation of Baku, both in 1918,
supplied the external pressures, and ideological
conflicts both within the Musavatists themselves
and between the Musavatists, Mensheviks and
Bolsheviks contributed to the instability of the
new government. The government, torn by internal
dissension, fell to the XIth Red Army and, on 28
May 1920, a Soviet government was established in
Baku.
The process of the Bolshevist takeover had
begun two months earlier when elements of the
Hummat and Adalat parties allied themselves with
the Azerbaijan organization of the Communist
Party of Russia(Bolshevik) and merged to form the
nucleus of the Azerbaijan Communist Party
(Bolshevik). The merger was the result of a
compromise between those advocating a separate
Communist party for Muslims and those advocating
a party based on class and territory. Due to
Azerbaijan's geopolitical position, it was felt
that some form of relationship with Russia was
inevitable; hence, the compromise reached was
felt to be the most palatable one(25).
Policies espoused by the new government led
to the development of many of the trappings of
the XXth century nation-state, both in terms of

institutions (such as the establishment of a
Commissariat of Foreign Affairs) and in basic
reforms directed at awakening and stimulating an
acceptable(to the Bolsheviks) form of Azerbaijani
national consciousness. Over the long term, the
most important of these reforms were language
reforms directed at bringing the Azeri literary
language in line with actual usage and the study
of the Azerbaijani past in order to establish and
codify it in line with the demands of party and
state. It should be noted that language reform
and the search for a national identity were both
movements which had begun in the mid-XIXth century; steps taken by the Soviet government were
merely continuations of well-established trends.

A consequence of these national cultural
policies was that a well-defined sense of
Azerbaijani nationhood began to take shape; not
all of it, however, was politically acceptable
either internally or for export to Iranian
Azerbaijan. One scholar has concluded that in
this early period the Soviet regime "explicitly"
denied the Azerbaijanis the role of an advance
guard of the revolution in Iranian Azerbaijan due
to the dangers of nationalist infection(26).

During this same period in Iranian
Azerbaijan, power was being wielded by Sheykh
Khiyabani's Azerbaijan Democratic Party which,
while vaguely social-democratic in nature,
basically advocated Muslim reforms and
modernization to make it more compatible with
constitutional government. In Soviet eyes, an
Islamic movement coupled with nationalism has
always posed a serious threat. Azerbaijan in
1920-1921 became merely a staging area for Soviet
adventures mounted against Iran.

Soviet Experiences in Iran: 1920-1921

Soviet attempts to influence and take over
revolutionary movements in Iran were failures for
various reasons, primary among which was a faulty
assessment of the readiness of the peoples in
Iran to support a Soviet style revolutionary
movement. The two major examples of this were the
Soviet efforts to take over the fate of the Gilan
Soviet Republic and to subvert Sheykh Khiyabani's
Azerbaijan Democratic Party.

In Gilan the Jangal movement of Mirza Kuchuk
Khan had been actively fighting against British
and Tsarist intervention in Iran since 1916. This
movement, also called Ittihad-i Islam[Islamic
Union], advocated the ousting of all foreign
powers from Iran, the overthrow of the dictator-
ship in Tehran and the establishment of a government based on an ill-defined mixture of social-
democratic and Muslim principles.

Following the temporary Bolshevik victory in
Azerbaijan in 1918, Kuchuk Khan sent a delegation
to Baku to plead for Soviet support for his
movement. While he received promises of help from
the Lankaran Committee of the Communist Party of
Russia(Bolshevik), due to the Soviet withdrawal
from Azerbaijan and subsequent British occupation
of Baku in 1918, no immediate aid was forth-
coming. In 1920, however, the situation had
changed. In 1920 Soviet power had established
itself once again in the Transcaspian region and
when a Soviet fleet landed near Rasht at the port
city of Enzeli, Kuchuk Khan approached them again
and met with a Soviet delegation which had
accompanied the fleet (the delegation included
Ordzhonikidze and several members of the Adalat
Party).

Kuchuk Khan's primary point in his
discussions with the Soviet delegation was that
any revolutionary government in Iran would have
to distance itself from any form of overt
Communist propaganda due to the religious
fanaticism prevalent among the population. The
Soviets agreed to support a provisional revolutionary government headed by Kuchuk Khan and
promised that they would not intervene in Iranian
affairs(27). Trotsky, who was informed about the
content of these talks in Moscow, proposed that
any military support needed by Kuchuk Khan be
given in the name of the newly-formed Soviet
Azerbaijan Republic and that the fleet in Enzeli
fly the Azerbaijani flag(28). Shortly after the
conclusion of these talks, Kuchuk Khan's army of
Jangalists occupied Rasht, and a revolutionary
committee under his leadership declared the
establishment of the Gilan Soviet Republic.

The Soviet non-intervention agreement was
violated immediately, apparently in order to pave

the way for a Communist takeover of Kuchuk Khan's
government. The Communist Party of Iran held its
first congress in Enzeli in June 1920 and shortly
thereafter began to publish its newspaper
Kommunist under the editorship of the Azerbaijani Bolshevik Pishevari. To both support the
new Soviet republic and undermine Kuchuk Khan's
authority, Soviet troops were dispatched to Gilan
from Baku; they did not fly the Azerbaijani flag.
As a result of a Soviet putsch, Kuchuk Khan was
removed from office on 30 June 1920 and was replaced by members of the Central Committee of the
Communist Party of Iran.

The policies of the short-lived Gilan Soviet
government, which included regular attacks on the
Muslim clergy and a hasty redistribution of
land, alienated the local population. The signing
of the Soviet-Iran Treaty in 1921 effectively
ended Soviet support for the Gilan movement, and
its remnants were quashed by troops sent from
Tehran.

Despite the Iranian, rather than Azerbaijani
nature of the Gilan revolution, the fact remains
that the leading members of its leadership were
Azerbaijani, especially after the Communist Party
of Iran had taken over from the Jangalists. Early
critiques of the Soviet mistakes in Gilan tended
to omit mention of the Azeri role in the Communist Party of Iran(29); in the late 1970s and
early 1980s, however, Soviet historians began to
give greater emphasis to the importance of a
national, rather than territorial approach to
national liberation in Iranian Azerbaijan(30).

"Azadistan"
Sheykh Khiyabani had been active in Iranian
constitutional politics since 1905 and, through
frequent sojourns in the North Caucasus, Baku and
Tiflis, was well aware of the political reform
movements sweeping through Russia. The Azerbaijan
provincial organization of the Democratic party,
which he led, had been in contact with the Tabriz
Soviet of Soldiers and Citizens Deputies since
its establishment although it was not under the
Soviet's ideological influence. In 1918, after
the withdrawal of Ottoman troops from Tabriz, the
Azerbaijan provincial organization of the Demo-

cratic Party renamed itself the Azerbaijan Democratic Party. The party's platform, expressed
through the pages of its newspaper Tajaddod
(Renewal), advocated an end to foreign interventionism in Iran and promoted reforms directed
at protecting the interests of craftsmen, small
merchants, the intelligentsia, workers and
farmers. Khiyabani himself maintained what he
called a "middle line" which was "not left and
not right" and referred to it as the "idea of
renewal"(31).

By 1920 Sheykh Khiyabani's movement had
gained substantial public support in Tabriz,
Zenjan, Akhar, Khoy, Ardebil and other cities and
towns of Iranian Azerbaijan. Finding the central
government in Tehran unresponsive to its political goals, the Azerbaijan Democratic Party convened a meeting in Tabriz and, on 22 June 1920,
passed a resolution to establish a national
government. The next day, a government headed by
Khiyabani and calling itself "Azadistan"(Land of
the Free") was announced in Tajaddod.

"Azadistan" only lasted three months. While
Khiyabani's objectives received some recognition
in the Baku press(32), it received no material
support from the Soviet government. It was also
resistant to Bolshevik manipulations within
Iranian Azerbaijan itself; the CPI, for example,
was unable to make any inroads into territories
controlled by the Azerbaijan Democratic
Party(33).

While a Soviet historian was to assert many
years later that "facts show that the democrats
of Iranian Azerbaijan did not raise the question
of secession from Iran"(34) and Soviet reprints
of Khiyabani's speeches and articles quote him as
wishing to "establish a stable regime in
Iran"(35), it is clear that whatever Khiyabani's
ultimate goals, "Azadistan" was a de facto
secession from Iran. One of the reasons for the
lack of Soviet enthusiasm for Sheykh Khiyabani's
national, pan-Islamic movement was that its
success would pose a threat to the stability of
the recently-formed Soviet Azerbaijan. "Azadistan" was quickly perceived by Tehran as a
serious danger to the central government; the
Iranian army marched on Tabriz in September 1920,

dissolved the Azerbaijan Democratic Party and
executed Sheykh Khiyabani. Subsequently,
Khiyabani's legacy was to be revived in a more
palatable form to the Soviets, and he himself
depicted as a hero of Azeri national liberation.

The Soviet-Iran Treaty of 1921
The negotiation of the Soviet-Iran Treaty of
1921 primarily ended the first phase of Soviet
adventurism in Iran and laid the foundation for a
new onslaught on Iran's territorial integrity. As
a consequence of its ratification, support for
the Gilan Soviet Republic was withdrawn and many
members of the CPI regrouped in Baku. Article Six
of the treaty (described by one scholar as
"odious") permitted the Soviets to occupy northern Iran if they felt their southern borders were
threatened by an enemy. It is worth while to cite
the article in toto:

> In the event that attempts by third
> countries to carry out an expansionist
> policy on the territory of Persia by way of
> military intervention or to convert the
> territory of Persia into a base of military
> operations against Russia, or if they would
> pose a danger to the borders of the RSFSR or
> states allied with it, and if the Persian
> government, after a warning by the Russian
> Soviet Government is itself incapable of
> averting this danger, the Russian Soviet
> Government will have the right to bring its
> army into the territory of Persia in order
> to take the necessary measures in the
> interests of self-defense.(36)

This article led to the Soviet occupation of
northern Iran in August 1941 and the second phase
of the Soviet penetration of Iranian Azerbaijan.
This time, however, the Soviets were well
prepared.

NOTES

1. cf. Akademiya Nauk. Institut Vostoko-
vedeniya. Zarubezhnyy Vostok. Yazykovaya
situatsiya i yazykovaya politika. Spravochnik.
(Moscow, 1986), p. 191.
2. Javad Heyat, "Regression of Azeri
Language and Literature under the Oppressive
Period of Pahlavi and Its Renaissance after the
Islamic Revolution", First International
Conference of Turkic Studies, Bloomington,
Indiana, May 19-22, 1983, p. 1; the sources he
cites are: Iranian Armed Forces. A Geographic
Dictionary of Rural Dwellings in Iran(n.d.) and
Dr. M. Panaheian, Geographic Dictionary of the
Turks of the Land of Iran, 4v. (n.d.).
3. The general data on these early
migrations were drawn from the following sources:
I. Artamonov. Istoriya Khazar.(Leningrad, 1962),
p. 142ff.; Z. M. Bunyatov, "Novoye issledovaniya
po istorii Azerbaydzhanskogo gosudarstva
Sadzhidov", Azarbayjan SSR Elmlar Akademiyasynyn
Khabarlari: Tarikh, Falsafa, Huguq seriyasy,
1980/3, pp. 132-133; K. H. Menges. The Turkic
Languages and Peoples: An Introduction to Turkic
Studies (Wiesbaden, 1968), p 42; N. Z.
Gadzhiyeva. Tyurkoyazychnye Arealy Kavkaza
(Moscow, 1979), pp. 221ff.
4. cf. N. A. Baskakov. Vvedeniye v
izucheniye tyurkskikh yazykov, 2nd ed., (Moscow,
1969), pp. 265-267 and Menges. op.cit., p. 60.
5. Aydyn Mammadov Adabiyyat va Injasanat 15
May 1984 p. 4.
6. A. K. Alekperov, "'Problemy istorii
Azerbaydzhanskogo yazyka'", Sovetskaya
Tyurkologiya, 1984/2, p. 108.
7. The "One Azerbaijan" slogan, which began
to appear in Soviet Azeri media in the 1980s,
signifies that not only are the Azeris of Iran
part of the Azerbaijani nation, but so is the
land on which they live.
8. Sh. A. Taghyyev, "Muasyr Iran burzhua
tarikhshunasyghynda Azarbayjan Khalginin etnik
birliyinin inkar edilmasi haggynda", Protiv
burzhuaznykh fal'sifikatorov istorii i kul'tury
Azerbaydzhana (Baku, 1978), p. 121.

24

9. cf. Kh. M. Ibragimbeyli in <u>Voprosy Istorii</u>, 1978/11, p 162.

10. Richard Frye. <u>Iran</u> (New York, 1953), p. 53.

11. M. M. Aliyev, "Ba'zi Iran matbuat organlary sahifalarinda Azarbayjan khalgi va onun manshayi masalalari", <u>Protiv burzhaznykh fal'sifikatorov...</u>, pp. 206-207; he is quoting Rezazade Shafag.

12. <u>ibid.</u>, p. 211.

13. A complete and succinct account of these two campaigns can be found in Sir Percy Sykes, <u>History of Persia,</u>II (London, 1963), pp. 311-322.

14. <u>Azarbayjan Tarikhi,</u>II (Baku, 1964), p. 49.

15. Schapour Ravasani. <u>Sowjetrepublik Gilan: Die Sozialistische Bewegung in Iran seit Ende des 19. Jhdt. bis 1922</u> (Bonn, n.d.), p. 116.

16. N. K. Belova, "Ot otkhodnichestva iz severo-zapadnogo Irana v kontse XIX nachale XX veka", <u>Voprosy Istorii</u>, 1956/10, pp. 113,117.

I7. Vladimir Minorskiy, "Dvizheniye persidskikh rabochikh", <u>Sbornik konsul'skikh doneseniy Ministerstva Inostrannykh Del,</u>III (St. Petersburg, 1905), p. 204ff.

18. Ravasani, <u>op.cit.</u>, p 125.

19. <u>Azarbayjan Tarikhi,</u> II, p 277.

20. Tadeusz Swietochowski, "The Himmat Party: Socialism and the National Question in Russian Azerbaijan 1904-1920", <u>Cahiers du Monde Russe et Sovietique,</u>xix, janv.-juin 1978, p. 119.

21. The organization of the <u>Ijtimaiyyun-Amiyyun</u> remains unclear. Some modern Soviet historians claim its name is synonymous with that of the <u>Mujahid</u>; others claim it was not. cf. Ye. I. Chapkevich. <u>Bol'sheviki i burzhuaznyye revolyutsii v Azii nachala XX v.</u> (Moscow, 1985) pp. 41-43.

22. G. S. Arutyunian. <u>Iranskaya Revolyutsiya 1905-1911 gg i bol'sheviki Zakavkaz'ya</u> (Yerevan, 1956), p. 121.

23. cf. Aziz Sharif's interesting memoir "Atam va man", Azarbayjan, 7/1980, p. 96ff. He noted that he and many others had done substantial organizational work in Tabriz prior to 1920 for the Nakhchyvan Soldiers and Workers Soviet. Although he had promised to give more data on this experience in the next installment of his memoirs, for some reason it was omitted.

24. Sh. A. Tagiyeva, "Sheykh Mokhammad Khiyabani i natsional'noye-osvoboditel'noye dvizheniye v Iranskom Azerbaydzhane v 1917-1920 gg.", Iran: Istoriya i sovremennost': Sbornik statyey(Moscow, 1983), pp. 109-110.

25. Swietochowski, op.cit., pp 130-132.

26. S. Enders Wimbush, "Divided Azerbaijan: Nation Building, Assimilation and Mobilization Between Three States", Soviet Asian Ethnic Frontiers (New York, 1979), pp. 67-68.

27. N. K. Belova, "K voprosu o tak nazymayevoy sotsial-demokraticheskoy partii Irana", Voprosy istorii i literatury stran zarubezhnogo Vostoka (Moscow, 1960), p. 24.

28. Ravasani, op.cit., pp. 287-288.

29. i.e. Irandust, "Voprosy Gilyanskoy revolyutsii", Istorik-Marksist, V/1927, p. 134ff.

30. Azeri revolutionary activists who were members of the Gilan Soviet government or played prominent roles in the Communist Party of Iran(CPI) during the 1920s are occasionally highlighted in the recent Soviet Azeri press: Z. Aliyev was noted as a member of the Gilan revkom in Kommunist, 8 December 1981, p. 4; M. J. Aghayev is mentioned as chairman of the Gilan Province Committee of the CPI during 1920-1921 in Kommunist, 15 April 1923, p. 4; Pishevari as Gilan Foreign Minister in Adabiyyat va Injasanat, 15 July 1983, p. 4; I. A. Akhundov as "party chekist" in Soviet-occupied Iran in 1920 in Kommunist, 3 February 1984, p. 4; and B. I. Aghayev as a minister in the Gilan government in 1921 in Kommunist, 29 August 1984, p. 4. Mirza Kuchuk Khan, also an Azerbaijani, is rarely mentioned in contemporary Soviet research.

31. Sh. A. Tagiyeva, "Sheykh Mokhammed Khiyabani...", p. 112.

32. Tagiyeva cites Kommunist(Baku) of 6 July 1920 to the effect that Khiyabani's government was ruled by "democratic principles", ibid., p. 117.

33. Ravasani, op.cit., p 356.

34. Tagiyeva, op.cit., p 117.

35. i.e., "Khiyabaninin nitglarindan", Azarbayjan, 5/1983, p. 82.

36. M. I. Volodarskiy. Sovety i ikh yuzhnyye sosedy. Iran i Afganistan: 1917-1933. (London, 1985), pp. 82-83.

3

The Red Army's Occupation of Iran and the Azerbaijan Democratic Republic

Introduction
     The signing of the Soviet-Iran Treaty in
1921 effectively ended the first phase of Soviet
involvement in Iranian internal affairs. From
1922 until 1941, overt relations between the two
states were primarily those of trading partners;
Soviet covert operations in Iran were directed
primarily at Great Britain and, to a lesser
degree, to maneuvers against movements such as
the Armenian Brotherhood, the Musavatists and
Russian anti-Soviet groups which were making an
effort to overthrow the new Bolshevik
government(1).
     Of greater interest were internal
developments in Iranian and Soviet Azerbaijan. In
Soviet Azerbaijan, the national consolidation
which had begun to take shape in the late 19th
century continued to develop. The most important
elements in this process were language and alphabet reforms, which not only served to bring an
end to illiteracy, but also made state propaganda more accessible to the population. Coupled
with this, a state-sponsored campaign to promote
a form of Marxist-Leninist national awareness was
quite effective. Under its aegis, Azerbaijan
began to undergo a cultural revival; literary
works which had fallen into obscurity were revived and given broad dissemination through the
educational system and the mass media; state
institutions, ministries and other public
organizations began to assume a kind of Azer-

baijani reality although they were, in fact, replicas of those developing in other national republics of the Soviet Union. This sense of national self-awareness was strong enough to survive the Stalin purges of the late 1930s in which many of the most prominent members of the Azeri intelligentsia, political as well as cultural, were swept away. By the outbreak of World War Two, it is safe to say that Soviet Azerbaijan had acquired a national identity.

In Iranian Azerbaijan the situation was quite different. Neither the Tabriz Constitutional movement under Sattarkhan (1908-1909) nor Khiyabani's 'Azadistan' had led to any kind of Azeri national cohesiveness in Iran; under current Soviet thinking, however, it is thought that these movements were important initial steps in the formation of Azeri national awareness in Iran(2).

After the collapse of the Qajar dynasty in Iran in 1925, the new government under Reza Shah adopted a strong centralistic policy with marked anti-Azeri overtones. One of the primary reasons for this orientation was the fear of the Soviet threat to its northern borders and the possibility that Azeri separatists would exploit this to achieve their own ends. To nip this potential threat in the bud, the use of Azeri in Iranian schools was forbidden. A contemporary Soviet nationality specialist has noted that this policy was directed at "the extirpation of the Azeri language, the assimilation of the Azeris and their isolation from the population of neighboring Soviet Azerbaijan"(3). In retrospect, these policies served to strengthen the Azeri national opposition to the Pahlavi regime.

The Communist Party of Iran fared no better. Meeting in Urmiya in 1927, it had called for the overthrow of the monarchy and the establishment of a revolutionary, federative, independent republic in Iran. In 1931, the CPI was banned and most of its Central Committee imprisoned. Protest from the Soviet Union was muted.

Iran's decision to embrace Aryanism as a state ideology and its growing relationship with Nazi Germany in the mid 1930s led to growing suspicions in the Soviet Union that Germany could

use Iranian territory as a springboard for the
invasion of the USSR. This suspicion led to the
second phase in the Soviet penetration of Iranian
Azerbaijan; unlike the first, which was characterized primarily by Soviet ignorance of Iranian
internal affairs which drew them into the short-
lived adventure in Gilan, the Soviets were well
prepared for the situation which confronted them
in Iran.

The "Military Orientalists" of the Red Army and the Occupation of Iran

The Japanese attack and occupation of Man-
churia in 1931 had alerted the Soviet Union to
the vulnerability of its own borders. In order to
prepare themselves for the eventuality of war on
its eastern and southern borders, a decree was
passed by the Central Committees of the Communist
Party and the Comsomol ordering the mobilization
of students at Soviet higher schools for training
in oriental studies. Special area and language
training courses were worked out for these students jointly by the Committee on Higher Education and the Peoples Commissariat of Defense.
The purpose of this training was "to prepare
specialist-orientalists (translators and analysts) who have mastered the necessary knowledge
in the fields of history, economics, economic
geography, sociology and ethnography, but mainly
those who have acquired the necessary linguistic
preparation for service and work in the staff and
units of the Red Army"(4).

While the first cadres were trained
primarily in Japanese and English, by 1938
specialists had been trained in the languages of
China, Korea, Turkey, Iran and Afghanistan. In
1940 GUPP (Chief Administration for Political
Propaganda of the Red Army) took over management
of these programs. GUPP's objective was "the
organization and conduct of propaganda with the
goal of undermining the moral-psychological
potential in armies of the true opponents of the
USSR, and preparations for the conduct of
propaganda and counterpropaganda in the armies
and among the population behind the front in the
event of war waged by imperialistic states
against our country"(5).

In June 1941 Germany invaded the Soviet Union. This had immediate consequences in Iran. A Soviet diplomat who was serving in Tehran at this time described the situation as it was then perceived by the Soviet leadership: "A fascist German 'fifth column' with spies and saboteurs in all provinces of Iran was activated. It was especially strong in Tehran and the northern provinces bordering on the USSR. In connection with this, our diplomats demanded from Reza Shah and his government that they take effective measures to eliminate this great danger to the southern borders of the USSR by expelling from Iran the Hitlerite spies and terrorists who were threatening the security of Iran and the USSR"(6).

Three notes concerning the Nazi threat in Iran to the USSR were delivered to the Iranian government in accordance with the Soviet-Iran Treaty of 1921. When these failed to elicit a favorable response, the Soviet Union, citing Article 6 of the treaty, claimed that the Nazis were using Iranian territory as a staging area for an invasion of the USSR and moved the Red Army into northern Iran on 25 August 1941. At the same time Great Britain, acting to protect its oil interests, occupied southern Iran.

The Soviet Air Force, acting in concert with Soviet ground troops, dropped pamphlets into the Iranian territories the army was to hold; these contained the Note of the Soviet government to the Shah of Iran and an Appeal by the Soviet Command to the Iranian People. On 25 August a brigade commissar of the Transcaucasian Military District reported that "aircraft of the 135th, 245th, 26th, 133rd and 134th air divisions distributed 1.1 million copies of the note and appeal. All military units entering Iran have been provided with these documents for distribution to the population along the way of march"(7). All in all, some 15 million copies of the appeal and note were dropped or delivered in northern Iran; of these, 11 million were in Azeri and Persian, 4 million in Armenian and 200 thousand in French.

Once the Red army had established itself, counterpropaganda units directed their work at

dispelling rumours that the army had entered Iran
to "establish Soviet power", abolish and per-
secute Islam and "collectivize" women. To this
end, the orientalists of GUPP held meetings, gave
lectures, made regular reports over loudspeakers
and radio points on the Soviet Union and Red
Army, and founded the Iran Society for Cultural
Relations with the USSR(8).

The Red Army in Iranian Azerbaijan

Virtually every aspect of the current Soviet
tactical approach to the Azeris of Iran can be
traced back to the experience of the Red Army,
especially the Soviet Azeri contingents of GUPP.
The primary reason for this is that many of the
Soviet participants in this action played major
roles in defining Soviet strategies and tactics
towards Iranian Azerbaijan in the postwar period.
The political administration of the occupied
areas was under the control of the GPU (Chief
Political Administration of the Red Army). A
ranking Soviet GPU officer claimed that "undoubtedly, the arrival of the Red Army in Iran
and the broad dissemination of Soviet friendly
and peaceful propaganda and information among the
Iranian people contributed the the development of
the democratic movement in the country"(9). In
view of developments in Iranian Azerbaijan, his
claim may be considered a major understatement.

Roughly six months after the Red Army's
occupation of Iranian Azerbaijan, a delegation of
Soviet Azeri political activists headed by Aziz
Aliyev, a secretary of the Central Committee of
the Azerbaijan Communist Party, and Mehbaly
Gasumov, a Moscow-trained specialist in XIXth
century Azeri intellectual history, visited
Tabriz at the invitation of the Red Army command.
While the content of discussions is unknown, one
consequence of the visit was that a special
Soviet Azeri GUPP unit was formed in order to
establish and develop contacts with the local
Iranian Azeri population: in a recent memoir
Mirza Ibrahimov, a member of this unit, described
its functions as follows:

Since there were a great many Azeri soldiers
in the part of Southern Azerbaijan we

occupied, we were to conduct propaganda and agitation work with them as well as to help cement the friendly relations which had been established from the very first days between the local population and our troops.(9)

It is worthy of note that in the months following the Soviet occupation, the CPI, which had been underground since 1931, re-emerged as the Peoples Party of Iran, and in Iranian Azerbaijan a number of organizations of a "revolutionary-democratic" nature sprang up(10). For the next several years, the Iranian Azeris were directly exposed to a major Soviet campaign aimed at developing their sense of national consciousness and in indoctrinating them into the virtues of the Soviet way of life. The most important weapon in this propaganda arsenal was a newspaper published in Tabriz in Azeri in the Arabic script, Vatan Yolunda(11); its first editor was Mirza Ibrahimov who was to become the major architect of the postwar Soviet approach to Iranian Azerbaijan.
In a retrospective view of the role of Vatan Yolunda Mirza Ibrahimov somewhat self-servingly described its impact in the following manner:

> For the Southern Azeris for whom schools, the press and literature in the mother tongue were banned, and who had been exposed to oppression and persecution through the denial of their identity, nationality, history, culture and language under the severe social and national tyranny of Reza Shah's despotism, Vatan Yolunda shone like a light in the darkness.(12)

Soviet Azeri culture also had an impact on other sectors of Southern life. Under Aziz Aliyev's recommendation a Soviet hospital and school were opened in Tabriz, theater and musical circles were organized and Soviet opera and ballet companies performed regularly in the cities of Iranian Azerbaijan. Emphasizing the impact of these measures some forty years after the fact, Ibrahimov wrote that "the uplifting spirit, the feelings of joy and appreciation

these beautiful meassures awakened among the
workers and intellectuals of Southern Azerbaijan
are indescribable"(13).

The Soviet staff of Vatan Yolunda actively
courted the "progressive" intelligentsia of
Tabriz and invited their participation in the
work of the newspaper. The full effects of this
collaboration, however, were not to be felt until
the postwar period. Political developments, the
most important of which was the establishment of
the Azerbaijan Democratic Republic, soon over-
shadowed the cultural revival in Iranian Azerbaijan.

The Formation of the Azerbaijan Democratic Republic

On 3 September 1945 the Azerbaijan
Democratic Party(ADP) was founded in Tabriz. Two
days later the Azerbaijan Province Committee of
the Iran Peoples Party(Tudeh) merged with it. By
giving the Marxist-Leninist ADP the same name as
Sheykh Khiyabani's "neither left nor right" party
of some 25 years earlier, the Soviets had taken
their first steps into the management of the
Iranian Azeri historical past in order to mani-
pulate its future. The overt objectives of the
ADP were to establish the autonomy of Azerbaijan
within Iran, to conduct the work of all schools
and state institutions in the Azeri language, to
redistribute the land and to limit the workday to
eight hours. Seyid Jafar Pishevari, who had been
released from an Iranian prison with the arrival
of Soviet occupation forces in Iran, was named
chairman of its Central Committee.

Despite statements directed at attaining
national autonomy within Iran, the Central
Committee immediately opted to move in the
direction of national independence. Following a
public appeal to "diplomatic officials from
democratic states and Iranian personnel" in which
atrocities allegedly committed against the Azeris
by the central government in Tehran were enum-
erated, it was claimed that the Iranian Army was
threatening to exterminate the Azeri nation(14).
How they were to do this with the Red Army in
place was never clarified.

On 9 November 1945 a plenum of the ADP's
Central Committee passed a resolution calling for
an armed struggle for the establishment of a
people's government. Since there was basically no
army to fight, it is clear that any military
action undertaken would have to have been undertaken against tribal elements, landlords and
Muslim clergy who were resisting the Soviet-
ization of Iranian Azerbaijan. At this time,
membership in the ADP had reached 70,000(15).

On 12 December an Azerbaijan National
Congress was convened in Tabriz and a government
formed by Pishevari, who was named Prime
Minister; for a brief period he had been Minister
of the Interior in the Gilan Soviet Republic.
Another member of the government, Jevdet, who was
named Deputy President of the National Assembly,
had also served in Gilan as Minister of Culture.

In the brief life of the Azerbaijan
Democratic Republic the only institution which
began to develop was the press, also under Soviet
guidance. While Vatan Yolunda continued publication as before, a periodical under Soviet
management but with many contributions from
Iranian writers and journalists, took over many
of its functions. Named Azarbayjan, its con-
tributors discussed many of the themes which were
to become focal points in Soviet national liberation tactics over the next forty years. In
effect, a structure of national symbols was beginning to evolve which were to be used in the
postwar period in the literature of "longing" and
Soviet and Iranian Azeri national unity. These
can be dated to efforts by the Azeri orientalists
of GUPP to create a Southern Azeri literature of
patriotism. An early essay by one of the editors
of Vatan Yolunda noted the success of this
tactic:

> The feeling of patriotism is developing from
> day to day. Poets who earlier wrote minor
> poems have begun to write great epics about
> the fatherland, Tabriz and Sattarkhan; they
> have joined the great struggle for the
> felicity of the fatherland with unswerving
> will.(16)

After the fall of the Azerbaijan Democratic
Republic in 1946, many of these progressive poets
fled to the Soviet Union where they were to play
major roles in keeping the "Southern question"
alive and participate in the further development
of the national liberation symbolism. The primary
approaches to this question were directed at
giving the Iranian Azeri population the impression that they were heirs to a major national
tradition. To this end, mythological and historical personages common to both Caucasian and
Iranian Azerbaijan were played up and given
"progressive" attributes. The Araz River, which
forms a part of the border between the two Azerbaijans, acquired great national liberation significance because it could be viewed both as a
symbol of Azeri unity and Azeri separation. This
was also initially introduced through the pages
of Azarbayjan. A Southern Azeri folklorist placed
it in a national liberation context when he described a children's game wherein the children
stand on each others' shoulders on the southern
bank of the Araz and look longingly northward. He
interpreted the origin of the game by noting that
"in 1243(1828) the other side of the Araz, our
northern compatriots, were given to the Russian
state by the Treaty of Turkmanchay"(17) and
stressed the separation of the Azerbaijani
people and their longing for unity. A verse from
the modern Soviet Azeri poet Kamran Mehdi demonstrates its symbolic flexibility:

> True, the Araz divides a nation,
> But the earth underneath is one!...(18)

On 1 May 1946 the Red Army began its
withdrawal from northern Iran. The Azerbaijan
Democratic Republic lingered on only a few more
months before the central government in Tehran,
"buttressed by the military power and moral support of the USA and other imperialistic powers",
fell to the Iranian Army(19).

Military Service in Iranian Azerbaijan: Its Impact on the Soviet Azeri Cultural and Political Intelligentsia

By all accounts, working on the staff of Vatan Yolunda had a major impact on the subsequent careers on the lives of Soviet Azeris assigned to it by GUPP during the war; since most of them were also members of the creative intelligentsia the success of works drawing on and inspired by their experiences there also had a resonance on the All-Union level. Suleyman Rustam, now considered to be the greatest poet of Soviet Azerbaijan, has stressed the influence of his Vatan Yolunda experiences in Iran on his later work(20); immediately after the war, in fact, his book of poetry Iki Sahil ("Two Banks"), which refers to the northern and southern banks of the Araz River, won a Soviet State Prize in 1947, and his epic poem Tabrizda Gysh ("Winter in Tabriz") was voted one of the best poems of the year by the Moscow literary journal Ogonyok in 1949(21).

Another writer connected to Vatan Yolunda, the playwright Anvar Mammadkhanly, was also strongly influenced by his experiences in Iranian Azerbaijan. In a recent discussion of his play Od Ichinda ("Under Fire"), which is concerned with the national liberation movement in Iranian Azerbaijan, a critic pointed out that "the Great Fatherland War and Tabriz marked a new period" in Mammadkhanly's life(22).

Jafar Khandan, Mirza Ibrahimov's successor at Vatan Yolunda, emerged in the postwar period as the major theorist on the application of symbolism to the Southern Azeri national liberation movement. His dissertation, defended at the Azerbaijan State University in 1949, was entitled "The Ideas of the National Liberation Movement in the Literature of Southern Azerbaijan"; in it, he traces the movement back to Sattarkhan and Sheykh Khiyabani and analyzes its evolution until 1946. It is now considered to be the "first scientific study" of themes relevant to Azeri national liberation literature(23).

Mirza Ibrahimov's work at Vatan Yolunda was only a prologue to his postwar role as a champion of the Southern Azeri cause. A number of his

essays had found a following among the "progressive" intelligentsia of Iranian Azerbaijan;
these stressed elements common to the Azeris of
the USSR and Iran and promoted patriotic,
national themes in Iranian Azeri literature(24).
His appointment to the post of Peoples Commissar
of Education AzSSR in 1942 in no way blunted his
efforts on behalf of Iranian Azeri national
liberation. His postwar novel The Coming Day
draws heavily on his experiences and impressions
gained while serving in Tabriz; it is now considered on of the greatest Soviet novels of
national liberation.

The staff of Vatan Yolunda had the
opportunity to study the situation of the Azeris
of Iran at close range and, on the basis of the
experience they gained, were able to develop a
literary program designed to buttress the
incipient nationalism of the Iranian Azeris in
subsequent years. The end result was that they
were able to control the development of a literature which communicated the inevitability of a
rapprochement between the two Azerbaijans couched
completely in terms of reference acceptable to
Soviet political objectives. Literary symbols
implying a common past and natural unity of
Soviet and Iranian Azerbaijan widely used in the
1980s were all developed during the Soviet occupation. This "literature of longing"(25) as it
is now called in the Soviet Union, has become a
dominant school in Soviet Azeri writing and is
used widely in Radio Baku broadcasts directed to
Iranian Azerbaijan in the 1980s(26).

NOTES

1. Soviet efforts against these movements
were directed by OGPU, a precursor to the modern
KGB; cf. the memoir by Georges Agabekov in OGPU,
(New York, 1931), especially pp. 73ff.
2. R. A. Seidov, "O natsional'nom
formirovanii Azerbaydzhantsev v Irane", Voprosy
natsional'no-osvoboditel'nogo dvizheniya na
Blizhnem i Srednem Vostoke, (Baku, 1985). p. 56.
3. ibid., p. 61.

38

4. B. G. Sapozhnikov, "Gotovnost' sovetskikh vostokovednykh kadrov k zashchite rodinu", Oruzhiyem slova: 1941-1945[henceforth: OS], p. 14.

5. ibid., pp. 23-24.

6. D. S. Kommissarov, "Iran: vzglyad v trevozhnoye proshloye(iz vospominaniy vostokovedov)", OS, pp. 104-105.

7. M. I. Burtsev, "Boyevaya deyatel'nost' vostokovedov v politorganakh sovetskikh voysk v Irane", OS, p. 93.

8. ibid., pp. 95-99.

9. Mirza Ibrahimov, "Ujalyghyn hikmati", Azarbayjan, 5/1983, p. 96.

10. Seyidov, op.cit., pp 62-63. These included the "Anti-Fascist Committee", "The Iran-Soviet Friendship Society", "The Organization of Workers of Azerbaijan" and many others.

11. Vatan Yolunda was generally published every other day from late 1941 to early 1946; cf. Azarbayjan dovri matbuaty (1920-1970-ji illar) (Bibliyografiya), (Baku, 1979), p. 138.

12. Mirza Ibrahimov, op.cit., p. 96.

13. ibid., p. 96.

14. "Dovlat mamurlarynyn kandlarda yarandyglary faja'i ifsha etmak ichin Azarbayjan Dimokrat Firgasi tarafyndan Azarbayjan dimokrat dovlatlarinin diplomasi mamurlaryna va Iran silahiyyatdar magamatyna achyg maktub", Azarbayjan(a), I/3-4, October-November 1945, pp. 12-13.

15. Azarbayjan Sovet Ensiklopediyasy, I (Baku, 1976), p. 136.

16. Jafar Khandan, "Iran Azarbayjanynyn vatanparvar shairlari", Azarbayjan(a), 1, January 1946, p. 17.

17. Ali Akbar Saba, "Gushgu balabam", Azarbayjan(a), 1, January 1946, p. 17.

18. Kamran Mehdi, Adabiyyat va Injasanat, 12 August 1983, p. 4.

19. Seyidov, op.cit., pp. 70-71.

20. Suleyman Rustam, Adabiyyat va Injasanat, 30 May 1980, p. 6.

21. M. Arif(ed.). Azarbayjan Sovet Adabiyyaty Tarikhi,II (Baku,1967), pp. 50-52.

22. Kamil Valiyev, "Oz sozunun soraghynda", Azarbayjan, 3/1983, pp. 183-184.

23. Yashar Garayev, <u>Adabiyyat va Injasanat</u>, 9 May 1980, p. 6.

24. Jafar Khandan, "Mirza Ibrahimovun Janub movzulary", <u>Azarbayjan</u>, 10/1981, pp. 77-82; this article is a shortened version of one which appeared in 1946.

25. cf. David Nissman, "The Origin and Development of the Literature of 'Longing' in Azerbaijan", <u>Journal of Turkish Studies</u>, VIII(1984), pp. 199-207.

26. cf. Latif Huseynov, chief editor of the Southern Desk of Radio Baku, on the handling of this type of programming in <u>Adabiyyat va Injasanat</u>, 24 August 1984, p. 3.

4

The "Southern Question" in Postwar Soviet Azerbaijan

Introduction
       The collapse of the Azerbaijan Democratic
Republic forced both Moscow and Baku to reflect
on the future of Iranian Azerbaijan. A number of
factors added impetus to these concerns: Iran's
efforts to dismantle the Azeri national establishment which had begun to develop under Soviet
tutelage in the cities of Iranian Azerbaijan, the
arrival in Soviet Azerbaijan of a number of prominent 'progressive' political and cultural
emigres, and a flood of literary works on the
national liberation of Iranian Azerbaijan written
by Soviet Azeris who had played an active role in
establishing contacts with their Iranian counterparts during the occupation of Tabriz and other
cities of the South between 1941 to 1946. It was
during these early postwar years that the ground
rules for all subsequent public debates on Iranian Azerbaijan's future were laid.
       By November 1946 the Iranian Army had
succeeded in reoccupying northwestern Iran. A
standard Soviet literary history states the the
immediate consequences of this in Iranian Azerbaijan were that "in a short time, the achievements in the national cultural sector were
annihilated. Books published in the mother
tongue, folklore collections and the works of
modern writers and poets were burned indis-
criminately"(1).
       In the aftermath of the fall of the
Azerbaijan Democratic Republic many of its most

prominent activists sought and received refuge in
the Azerbaijan SSR. The Iranian Azeri literary
emigres were warmly received by the Azerbaijan
Writers Union, which organized public meetings
and forums at which Iranian and Soviet Azeri
writers presented the case for the national
liberation of Southern Azerbaijan. On 27 December
1947, for example, the Azerbaijan Writers Union
and the Azerbaijan Society for Cultural Relations
with Foreign Countries held a joint meeting at
which the achievements of Southern Azeri literature were discussed; similar meetings were to be
held throughout the next thirty years. Literary
works written by the emigration began to find
their way into print. Between 1948-1950 a number
of these received critical praise: these include
the 1948 literary anthology Tabrizin Sasi ("The
Voice of Tabriz"), Balash Azaroghlu's epic poem
Savalan (the name of a mountain in Iranian
Azerbaijan), a second anthology of Iranian Azeri
poetry, and books of verse by the poets Ali Tude
and Madina Gulgun, both of them still active
today. These works, and the publicity attendant
upon them, contributed to keeping the "Southern
question" in the public eye, at least in Soviet
Azerbaijan.

It was the work of Soviet Azeris who had
been involved directly with the the occupation,
however, that brought the "Southern question" to
the All-Union stage and established it as being
of future political significance. In this context, Mirza Ibrahimov's novel about the national
liberation movement in Iranian Azerbaijan was
perhaps the most important literary event in
postwar Soviet Azerbaijan.

"The Coming Day"
Mirza Ibrahimov's novel Galajak Gun ("The
Coming Day") was the first work to raise the
question of the national liberation of Iranian
Azerbaijan to the All-Union level. The history of
its writing also provides a good insight into the
processes through which such a work must pass in
order to find public and party approbation. An
early version of it appeared in the Baku literary
journal Ingilab va Madaniyyat in 1948; a revised
edition of it was published in book form in 1949,

and a Russian translation of the revised edition
appeared a year later after having gone through
yet another revision. In a review of the Russian
translation the critic Konstantin Fedin, noting
that he had followed the development of
Ibrahimov's work closely, wrote that "after the
first, native-language variant appeared in Baku,
Ibrahimov did an exceptional amount of work. This
was not only the result of his important collaboration with the editor and translator;
Ibrahimov did it because he wished to raise the
esthetic level of his work"(2).

Whatever the artistic quality of the book,
its appearance was to have lasting political
significance. The issues it raised and discussions it generated were to act as a major
stimulus and give direction to all future
developments in the Soviet treatment of the
"Southern question" up to the present day. Its
prestige and public were considerably augmented
when the novel was awarded the Lenin Prize in
1951.

The work's political relevance was
recognized even prior to its publication. An
examination of its earliest version, in 1946, led
Jafar Khandan to point out its "special place
among the works devoted to the South from the
point of view of the questions it encompasses and
its content"(3); Samad Vurghun, who had dominated
Soviet Azeri literary politics since the days of
the establishment of Soviet power claimed that
"it is one of the first major works to be devoted
to the heroic life struggle of the peoples of the
East for socialism and democracy in all of Soviet
literature"(4).

Soviet political-literary criticism recognized that Azerbaijani national consciousness is
given special emphasis in the novel. In a discussion centering around an analysis of the
motivation of Firidun, the protagonist of The
Coming Day, a Soviet literary history asserts
that

> Firidun is fighting not only for the
> liberation of the Azerbaijanis, but also for
> other peoples living in Iran. But his own
> people, their great culture and revol-

utionary past awakened a special feeling of
pride in Firidun. Because he understood the
important social and political events well
and because he was witness to the attitude
of superiority that the Persian chauvinists
held toward the culture and language of the
Azerbaijani people, his national consciousness, internationalism and humanism were
strengthened.(5)

In fact, one of the novel's strongest mes-
sages is that national consciousness is strengthened in adversity; in Soviet Azerbaijan where
many members of the creative and political
intelligentsia had been swept away by the purges
only a decade earlier, it was this element which
led to the novel's enduring appeal to the Soviet
Azeri readership.
    The great political importance attributed to
the novel at the time of its publication also
signaled a tactical change in the Soviet propaganda directed at Iran; the national question
had begun to take precedence over the class
struggle. This foreshadowed the great stress
placed on national liberation struggles by the
Soviet regime in the years following The Coming
Day's publication.
    It is worthy of note that at the time The
Coming Day was being rewritten to permit its
circulation on the All-Union level, another Azeri
work concerning Iranian Azerbaijan underwent the
same process. Mammad Said Ordubadi is now considered to be the first Soviet Azeri historical
novelist. Prior to the outbreak of World War Two
he had published the first parts of Dumanly
Tabriz ("Smoke-covered Tabriz") which focussed on
Sattarkhan, the military leader responsible for
the defense of Tabriz in 1908-1909 against the
central government during the Constitutional
movement in Iran. The last volume of his novel
was published in Baku in 1948. The novelist depicted Sattarkhan as faithful to the ideas of
constitutionalism, an individual who never acted
out of his own self-interest and as a fearless
and incorruptible political activist. Yet, in the
latter part of the novel, Sattarkhan began to
emerge as a character who "is not free of in-

decision and contradiction" and who was occasionally "weak and pale". Since these qualities
did not befit an historical personage who was
being groomed by the Soviet propaganda apparatus
as a hero of the Azeri national liberation
movement in Iran, the Russian translation of
Smoke-covered Tabriz was changed to eliminate
these shortcomings(6).

The rewriting of two novels on Iranian
Azerbaijan to make them more politically and
artistically acceptable for public consumption
demonstrates the importance of the "Southern
question" in Moscow. By the 1950s the issue began
to take on a wider dimension. Other state institutions began to establish departments which
dealt with certain aspects of national liberation
for the Azeris of Iran. It was only natural that
the chief spokesman for this movement came to
play a leading role in the management of this
question.

The Institutionalization of the "Southern Question" in the Azerbaijan SSR

In 1955 the Presidium of the USSR Academy of
Sciences passed a resolution converting the
Section of the History of Countries of the
Foreign East, which had been part of the
Institute of History of the Azerbaijan SSR
Academy of Sciences, into a "major center for
Iranian studies in our country"(7). This section,
upgraded to full institute status, was renamed
the Institute of Oriental Studies. Its functions
included the study of ways to develop national
liberation and revolutionary movements in the
countries of the Near and Middle East and to
assess the role of historical personages in this
question. In 1965 it was renamed the Institute
for the Peoples of the Near and Middle East.

An examination of research projects
undertaken by the institute staff on Iranian
questions reveals a number of monographs on the
working class and workers movements, Soviet-
Iranian relations, American imperialism in Iran
and the national liberation struggle in Iranian
Azerbaijan. It has had a section devoted exclusively to Iranian Azerbaijan at least since
1983(8).

In 1976 the Nizami Institute of Literature,
also under the Azerbaijan SSR Academy of
Sciences, formed a section for the "study and
publication of Southern Azerbaijani literature"(9) which has been headed by Mirza
Ibrahimov since its founding. Mention of this
section began to appear in the Azeri mass media
only after the fall of the Shah of Iran.

The development of academic departments
devoted to the "Southern question" were
paralleled by developments in other public
sectors, of which the most important was Radio
Baku. While foreign broadcasts to Iran had been
made over the radio since 1941, programs directed
at a specifically Iranian Azeri audience did not
commence until the mid 1950s. Until 1979,
however, programs stressed the "analysis of life
in our republic, the achievements of socialism
and international affairs"(10); then these
broadcasts began to assume a more assertive tone
by promoting an active sense of Azeri national
awareness among their listeners in Iran. This
tactic was extremely successful; a Radio Baku
official noted that letters sent to the radio's
Southern Desk had "increased" since the fall of
the Shah(11).

Although seldom in public view, the
Azerbaijan Communist Party was an all-important
player in the elaboration of the "Southern
question". All Soviet Azeris who have been
prominent in this issue have been party members
and some have held, and hold important positions
on the All-Union level. Mirza Ibrahimov, for
instance, has been a party member since 1930 and
Chairman of the Soviet Committee for Solidarity
with Asian and African Countries since 1977. It
must also be remembered that a secretary of the
Central Committee of the Azerbaijan Communist
Party was one of those responsible for bringing
the Soviet Azeri cadres into Iranian Azerbaijan
under the aegis of GUPP in 1941. Dating from the
same period the Azerbaijan Communist Party has
been responsible for printing materials for Tudeh
for distribution in Iran, a function it continues
to the present day(12).

The Azerbaijan Writers Union occupies the
most visible position in discussions of the

"Southern question". There are a number of reasons for this: many current members were in Iran at the time of the Soviet occupation; a number of others emigrated to Soviet Azerbaijan after the fall of the Azerbaijan Democratic Republic; above all, the media are controlled to a great extent by the writers' union, thus many of the writers' concerns find their way into print more rapidly than the opinions of others. There is a natural close relationship between writers, especially poets, and the Azerbaijan State Television and Radio Committee which exploits their output for programming into Iranian Azerbaijan.

In the period following the fall of the Shah, roughly from 1979 onward, other in- stitutions, such as the AzSSR Ministry of Education and faculties of journalism in the higher schools, also added departments and course work devoted to various aspects of the "Southern question".

An examination of Soviet Azeri media shows that all of those writing about the future of the national liberation movement in Iranian Azer- baijan. Russian and other Soviet scholars have discussed only the more theoretical questions or issues concerned with developments in Iran as a whole. In the media of Soviet Azerbaijan, treat- ment of Iranian Azerbaijan is less ideological than it is national, and it is national in a sense that encompasses Iranian Azerbaijan as well as Soviet Azerbaijan. This becomes evident in Azeri media dating from 1979 onward.

The Soviet Efforts to Penetrate Iranian Azerbaijan: 1979-1981

In the two years following the overthrowal of the Shah Iranian Azerbaijan was virtually completely open to Soviet ideological penet- ration; this reached its apogee in 1981. In 1979 the ban on the use of the Azeri language in Iran was lifted and numerous Azeri-language public- ations -- newspapers, magazines and books -- began to appear in Tabriz, Ardebil, Tehran and other cities with large Azeri populations. The majority of these advocated that Iranian Azer- baijan be granted some form of cultural and

national autonomy within an Iranian state. In
order to exploit this tendency, Soviet institutions concerned with Iranian Azerbaijan stepped
up all operations dealing with propagandizing
cultural, linguistic and political directions
which would aid in the establishment of an Azeri
national identity in Iran on a mass level.

In 1979 and 1980 the Soviet Azeri academic
and literary communities apparently received
Moscow's go-ahead to emphasize two tasks:
firstly, to indoctrinate the Iranian Azeris with
a sense of their own nationality by stimulating
the development of the Azeri language; and
secondly, to reaffirm to Soviet Azeris the ad-
vantages of Soviet citizenship by making invid-
ious comparisons between their status and life in
the USSR and that of their co-nationals in Iran
under Pahlavi rule. By stressing the importance
of language, the Soviets hoped to both break the
hold of the Shahist pan-Iranian ideology on the
Iranian Azeri population and to draw a distinction between Azeri and Iranian national
interests. By stressing that life was better
under the Soviet system than the Iranian, Soviet
ideological authorities hoped to control possible
outbursts of nationalism in the Azerbaijan SSR
itself. Readers of the Soviet Azeri mass media
were constantly reminded of the atmosphere of
repression under which the Iranian Azeris had
been living for several decades.

Since the ultimate goal of this tactic was
to establish a bond of common nationality between
the Azeris of Iran and the Soviet Union, Soviet
media available in Iranian Azerbaijan, as well as
Iranian media which could manipulated by the
Soviets, were meticulously orchestrated with this
end in mind. The interaction between media organs
in Soviet Azerbaijan and Iran, on one hand, and
published individual statements of intent, on the
other, yield a clear and somewhat detailed pict-
ure of the first post-Pahlavi contacts between
Soviet and Iranian Azerbaijan.

The First Soviet Moves in Iran

The first major public statement on
developments in post-Pahlavi Iran appeared in an
essay by Mirza Ibrahimov entitled "Revival in the

South". Although it appeared in the literary
monthly of the Azerbaijan Writers Union, it was
clearly compiled by Ibrahimov's staff in the
Section for Southern Azeri Language and Literature at the Nizami Institute of Literature. The
essay cites numerous statements culled from post-
Pahlavi Iranian Azeri publications; these statements revealed the existence of a strong nationalist sentiment and a political tendency towards
cultural and political autonomy within an Iranian
context. The fact that many of the citations
quoted in the Ibrahimov essay were couched in a
terminology with an extremely Soviet flavor was
not unexpected, given the source. Ibrahimov
explained this to the Soviet Azeri readership by
claiming:

> The Azerbaijanis, like all peoples of Iran
> seeing the light of a revolutionary dawn
> after the dark night of fifty years of
> tyranny, have taken the first joyful steps
> on the road to educational, cultural,
> spiritual and social uplift. Long-suppressed
> aspirations of the people have begun to
> flourish and these are finding their
> expression, above all, in belles-
> lettres.(13)

Many of the works of poetry and prose cited
as examples of an Iranian Azeri national
awakening were written prior to the Iranian
revolution and, as such, complain about national
oppression and persecution under the Pahlavis or
extol the virtues of the Azeri language. These
were not published during the Shah's rule, and
only began to find their public after 1979. The
Iranian Azeri literary intelligentsia who had
found a haven in Soviet Azerbaijan, however, had
been stressing these same themes since 1948; this
led Soviet literary critics to point out that
Soviet and Iranian Azeri literature had followed
parallel paths of development in the postwar
period, despite the fact that none of the Iranian
Azeri literature had been published before
1979(14). The political significance of this
literary parallelism was interpreted to mean that
there were still Azeri writers in Iran working

along lines which had been espoused by Jafar
Khandan's Poets' Circle, which was organized by
the Soviet Azeri-language newspaper <u>Vatan
Yolunda</u> in Tabriz in 1944. The implications of
this situation were that there existed in Iran
Azeri cadres who were clearly not unwilling to
work with their Soviet counterparts in order to
receive national autonomy.

Iranian Azeri writers taking positions
closely akin to those advocated by the Soviets
are quoted extensively in the Soviet Azeri media.
M. E. Yashar, for example, is quoted as stating
in an Azeri journal published in Tehran in 1979
that the "'feudal-bourgeois chauvinists'" of the
Pahlavi period had created a situation in which
"'the people of Azerbaijan...were forbidden an
existence wherein they could use their mother
tongue, regional characteristics, national
awareness and culture'" as a result of which
"'their activities and skills were crushed and
liquidated because they could not follow a
healthy evolutionary path and their very best
human qualities were ridiculed'"(15). The same
statement could just as easily have been made in
Soviet Azerbaijan without any changes made by
political censors. This very selective manipulation of quotations emanating from post-
Pahlavi Iranian Azeri media characterizes the
Soviet public examination of the "Southern
question".

A good example of the Soviet coverage is the
treatment given to discussions on forming an
Azerbaijan Writers and Poets Association in Iran;
readers of the reportage printed in the Soviet
Azeri literary monthly were informed that the
proceedings were compiled from "materials in
Iranian journals"(16) and informed that Huseyn
Duzgun, the editor of the pro-Soviet Iranian
Azeri literary journal <u>Yoldash</u> ("Comrade"), had
called a meeting to discuss the formation of an
organization for Iranian Azeri writers. Among the
questions to be discussed he proposed the following: to form a writers' and poets' association
which would "communicate with other writers and
progressive organizations of the world"; to de-
fend the "honor of our literary heritage which
was almost destroyed by the depredations of the

Pahlavi regime"; to spread the concept of a
"toiling and working class" among the people,
while at the same time "distancing ourselves from
any kind of nationalistic or fanatical remedies";
to prepare "textbooks in the mother tongue for
the coming school year"; to acquaint the younger
generation with "our proud pedagogical and
literary heritage"; and to communicate "the basic
program of our association to the Persian-
language Tehran dailies"(17).

Duzgun also made more general political
demands, i.e., that the "provincial and regional
associations foreseen in the Constitutional
period" be revived in a "more progressive and
modern manner" and that "the state grant autonomy
to Azerbaijan"(18).

Despite the political nature of Duzgun's
proposals, however, subsequent discussions
revolved almost exclusively around language and
the role that the literary language of Soviet
Azerbaijan should play in the Azeri language
revival in Iran. The language issue was complex:
firstly, Soviet Azeri used a modified Cyrillic
script and Iranian Azeri a modified Arabic;
secondly, Soviet Azeri had under-gone a number of
language reforms while Iranian Azeri had been
banned for some 35 years which had precluded any
controlled development; thirdly, the literary
language of Soviet Azerbaijan was based primarily
on the dialect of Baku which is phonologically
and, to a certain extent, grammatically different
from that of Tabriz; fourthly, the language of
Soviet Azerbaijan was inextricably connected
with communism. On the other hand, Azeri scholars
had felt since the XIXth century that the Arabic
script was a barrier to literacy; also, the only
available dictionaries, grammars and textbooks
were Soviet products; finally, Soviet Azerbaijan
was willing to help. The Soviets, convinced that
the more language was discussed in Iranian Azerbaijan, the greater the development of an Azeri
national awareness, and the closer the two Azerbaijans would come together, made language the
focal point in their writing and broadcasts to
Iran.

Many facets of Duzgun's platform for
political and cultural change were echoed in the

demands of the non-Marxist <u>Anjumen-i Azerbaijan</u>
(Council of Azerbaijan) which also demanded autonomy in administrative, judicial, economic and
security affairs as well as in culture, language
and politics(19). It became clear, however, that
the language issue was one on which almost all
Iranian Azeris could agree, no matter what their
personal political or religious proclivities
might be. Mirza Ibrahimov quoted a "letter to the
editor" published in an Iranian Azeri political
magazine in which its author claimed that the
opposition to the Azeri language in Iran was a
"movement of those who wish to bind us by force
to their language and culture -- a satanic
rebellion against the will of Allah"(20). This
mass popular support for the Azeri language in
Iran provided the Soviets with a major propaganda
advantage.

In addition to numerous monographs and other
scholarly studies on language problems in Iranian
Azerbaijan, in 1979 two Soviet Azeri poets,
Bakhtiyar Vahabzade and Aliagha Kurchayly, had
canvassed Iranian Azeri students in England about
their aspirations for the future of Iranian Azer-
baijan(21). In the same year, Vahabzade broadcast his poem "Mother Tongue" to Iranian Azerbaijan over Radio Baku; his broadcast was re-
corded and the text of the poem was subsequently
reprinted in an Azeri journal in Tehran(22). When
Soviet readers had the opportunity to read the
poem, Vahabzade claimed it had been inspired by a
letter he had received from Iranian Azerbaijan
which he quoted as saying: "I am one of you; that
is, I am Azeri. Unfortunately, I do not know my
mother tongue. Please send me a textbook so I can
learn my language"(23).

On the same date as the Soviet publication
of Vahabzade's poem, another article in the same
newspaper noted that books were being collected
and sent to Iranian Azerbaijan under the auspices
of Ibrahimov's Section for Southern Azeri
Language and Literature(24).

The first responses to changes occurring in
Iranian Azerbaijan as a result of the ouster of
the Shah concentrated on the importance of re-
establishing the language and providing the
Iranian Azeris with the necessary material and

cultural support. National autonomy was only
mentioned as an Iranian Azeri demand.

The Iranian Azeri Emigration in the USSR and the Dual Fatherland Concept

The primary form of communication between
the Azeri emigres in the Soviet Union and their
co-nationals in the South was poetry. A leading
member of the Iranian Azeri emigre literary community in Baku, Balash Azeroghlu, explained that
this was because

> poetry occupied the leading position in
> Southern Azeri literature during the
> Constitutional period and during 1941-1946,
> and still does so today. Certainly, one of
> the important reasons for this is that
> poetry is capable of expressing events in
> life more adroitly [than prose] and can
> reflect them with precision...More im-
> portantly, the native language of the
> people, their national existence and
> mentality, their struggle and revolution
> conducted against the Pahlavi dynasty have
> been celebrated in this poetry.(25)

Four poets who had emigrated from Iranian
Azerbaijan to the Soviet Union in 1946 had
specialized in writing about the Shahist oppression of the Iranian Azeris and calling for
national liberation throughout their entire
Soviet careers: Balash Azeroghlu, Hokuma Billuri,
Madina Gulgun and Ali Tuda. Their role was to
establish a bond with the "progressive" poets in
the South by initiating a public dialogue and
"longing" in print for their former homeland in
the literary press and mass media. Since Soviet
Azeri newspapers and magazines had begun to cir-
culate widely in Iranian Azerbaijan after the
fall of the Shah, many of these poems received a
warm response from like-thinking writers in
Tabriz. Hokuma Billuri introduced one of her
"longing" poems by saying "in Tabriz they spread
word I was dead". The poem elicited a response
from an Iranian Azeri poet which was repinted in
the Baku literary press alongside her orig-
inal(26). The poet Ali Tuda "longed" for Southern

Azerbaijan four times in the Soviet press between
August 1980 and May 1981(27). As Iranian and
Soviet sources from this period attest, the
Soviet plan for initiating a nationally-oriented,
public dialogue between Soviet and Iranian Azeri
writers was achieved through the use of the
Southern Azeri literary emigration.

The Soviet Azeri media actively solicited
reader and listener responses from their audience
in Iranian Azerbaijan. Ali Tuda noted in passing
that since the Baku literary newspaper had been
writing about Iranian Azerbaijan, it had received
many letters "from the other side of the
Araz"(28). Very often these letters were published in the press accompanied by an introduction from a prominent emigre. It is unclear
whether these letters were mailed directly from
Iran to Baku or whether they were sent by other
means.

The emigration, of course, did not fail to
express its gratitude for the support of the
Azerbaijan Communist Party. At the 7th Congress
of Soviet Azerbaijani Writers in 1981 Balash
Azeroghly, who had just been awarded the honor-
ific title "people's writer of Azerbaijan" a
month earlier, said in his speech:

> A number of writers who came from Southern
> Azerbaijan have chosen a second fatherland
> in Soviet Azerbaijan. All of us are deeply
> grateful to the Central Committee of the
> Azerbaijan Communist Party and the govern-
> ment of the republic for establishing every
> condition for creative productivity here so
> that we can create works which can help in
> the just struggle of our compatriots and
> brothers for freedom and social
> progress.(29)

The "second fatherland" concept proved to be
somewhat awkward when expressed poetically. One
poet says: "I know I am a strange bird: Tabriz a
fatherland, Baku a fatherland"(30) and another
refers to "my this-side-that-side" or "my
wherever-the-fatherland-is"(31). This duality was
to be resolved soon after Azeroghlu's speech at
the Azerbaijan Writers Congress with the less

cumbersome and more all-encompassing "One Azerbaijan" slogan.

At the same congress the Soviet writer
Shamil Salmanov defined the function of the
literary emigration with regard to the "Southern
question"; stressing their importance in the
ideological struggle then taking place in Iranian
Azerbaijan, he said that in their work "we see an
attempt to examine to analyze the Southern
question not only on a political basis, but also
on a philosophical-social and historical
basis"(32).

In using the emigration to affect the way in
which the Iranian Azeri intelligentsia thought
about themselves, Soviet ideologists, by analyzing the Azeri media in Iran and searching out
any echoes of Soviet-sponsored national awareness, were able to assess the success or failure
of their efforts.

Soviet Analyses of National Cultural Developments in Iranian Azerbaijan

The Soviet Azeri intelligentsia were kept
informed of national trends and cultural
developments in the South. Works of "progressive" Iranian Azeri writers were reprinted often
in Soviet Azeri mass media; the Azerbaijan
Writers Union established a special department
for relations with Azeri writers in Iran; the
Ministry of Education began to run a special
column in its own newspaper to keep secondary
school teachers informed on developments in
Iranian Azerbaijan. At first, publishing
activity in Iran was at the center of attention.

Between 1979-1981 virtually all Azeri
publishing activity in Iran met with Soviet
approval simply because it contributed to the
revival of the language. The major Azeri publishing centers were in Tabriz and Tehran: in
these and a number of smaller cities in Iranian
Azerbaijan numerous literary and political
journals and newspapers, which presented a
variety of ideas and views to their readers,
started publication. Politically, the same issue
of a journal would contain both radical and con-
servative approaches to the problem of Iranian
Azerbaijan's future. Most of these publications

were extremely short-lived; as one dropped from
sight, however, another would appear to replace
it. Yet the conflicting ideas they contained were
viewed positively by Soviet observers; Mirza
Ibrahimov likened the seemingly chaotic situation
in publishing to that which had existed in Russia
after the 1905 Revolution and even praised the
variety of ideas contained in their contents:

> Does this situation diminish the value of
> these works, or reduce their great value and
> influence in the cultural development of our
> people? Definitely not!...Our great public
> servants have been able to influence those
> strata and individuals in our society
> through the bourgeois and semi-landlord-
> oriented media...There is no reason to fear
> contradictions or utterances of people with
> different views and positions from our
> own.(33)

By the end of 1981, however, the Islamic
government began to strengthen its hold over
Iranian society; as a consequence, more and more
of the Iranian Azeri publications began to go
under and they were not replaced by others. By
the end of 1981 twelve Southern Azeri literary
and political journals had failed(34) and by the
end of 1984 only one magazine, Varlyq, had
survived. It is clear that Ibrahimov was somewhat
over-optimistic in his evaluation of the
political situation.
Yet, during the 1979-1981 period many Soviet
Azeri writers had contributed to these Southern
Azeri publishing efforts: poetry by Suleyman
Rustam, prose by Mirza Ibrahimov and all the
works of the Azeri exiles in Baku found a new
audience through the pages of these evanescent
Southern Azeri journals. While it was by no means
obvious in 1981, it would shortly become clear
that, apart from language, other factors such as
religion and politics were gaining in importance
in Iran.
The atmosphere of optimism about developments in Iranian Azerbaijan lasted at least to
1983. At an Azerbaijan Writers Union meeting
Sabir Amirov, who headed a special department

within the Writers Union to evaluate the extent
of Soviet influence appearing in the works of
Southern Azeri writers, maintained that
"socialism, which has established itself in the
north of the fatherland, has created its own
well-written, powerful, idealistic literature.
This literature has always been a literary school
for Southern writers"(35).

If the political content of Southern Azeri
literature was satisfactory to their Soviet
colleagues, the style and language were not. "No
matter how much we appreciate the content and
militant spirit of these works", Azeroghlu wrote,
"we also feel that many of them are still at a
low esthetic and artistic level. Certainly, these
languages mistakes and artistic shortcomings are
legacies [of the Pahlavi period]"(36).

The Soviet Azeri reader had the opportunity
to acquaint himself with carefully selected
poetry, short stories and essays from Iranian
Azeri publications which were reprinted in the
Baku literary media. Through reading this output,
one received the impression that there were any
number of writers in Iranian Azerbaijan who had
fallen under the influence of Soviet ideas about
the importance of the fatherland and the nation
of Azerbaijan. By the same token, the publicity
given the works of Soviet Azeri writers which
appeared in the Southern Azeri literary journals
only served to reinforce these impressions. That
all this was, to a certain extent, illusory only
became apparent later.

"Progressive" Writers of Iranian Azerbaijan

In order to be recognized as a "progressive"
writer in Iranian Azerbaijan, certain requirements had to be met. One must have been among
those who supported Azeri autonomy in Iran during
Pahlavi rule and, if a member of the older generation, an activist in political or literary circles during the Azerbaijan Democratic Republic.
With regard to those beginning their work after
the fall of the Shah, their literary output had
to meet the approval of the section in the
Writers Union whose responsibility it was to
evaluate its usefulness in attaining Soviet
objectives(37). Ideologically speaking, the

Azerbaijan Writers Union has defined a "progressive writer" as one who holds an "active life position" in which he is "promoting the ideals of communism"(38).

Soviet Azeri writers have spoken out very strongly on the characteristics of Southern Azeri "progressive" literature; in 1982 Mirza Ibrahimov, speaking in his capacity as chairman of the Writers Union, claimed that "progressive writers and poets in Iranian Azerbaijan are speaking out more and more against imperialism through poetry, prose and publicistic works...in democratically oriented journals in Tehran and Tabriz"(39). Their works focus on "the life of the working man, topics arising from the needs of the day, and the revolution and its heroes"(40).

While the Southern Azeri section in the Writers Union occupied itself with identifying progressive writers and topics, its equivalent in the Nizami Institute of Literature of the AzSSR Academy of Sciences was busy codifying the history of this movement. One of the fruits of its labors is the three-volume Anthology of Southern Azerbaijani Literature, the second volume of which, carries the works of many Iranian Azeri writers still active in Iranian literary life(41).

"Progressive" Publishing in Iran: 1979-1984
Azeri "progressive" publishing flourished in Iran only between 1979 and 1983. Its history is best exemplified by following the career of the Soviet-backed publicist, editor and poet Huseyn Duzgun (also known as Huseyn Sadig) who edited and published three magazines in succession during this period: Yoldash(Comrade), Ingilab Yolunda(On the road to revolution) and Yeni Yol(New road), organized the preliminary meeting of the Azerbaijan Writers and Poets Association, and founded the Azerbaijan Cultural Society. When he visited the Soviet Union in 1982, he was described as a person "who holds an active and serious position as a writer and poet in the revolution" and whose journal (then Ingilab Yolunda) "presents writers and poets of the Soviet Union, Soviet Azerbaijan and Soviet Turkmenistan to Iranian readers"(42).

Upon Duzgun's return to Iran, he began to publish Yeni Yol under the auspices of the Azerbaijan Culture Society. In its first issues he explained that his goal was "to publish mass scientific literary research materials"(43). A Soviet analysis of its second issue, noting that the lead editorial demanded that the Iranian Ministry of Education permit teaching in the Azeri language and that textbooks be printed for this purpose, pointed out that the journal's literary content revealed "the spirit of hatred, anger and struggle against American imperialism, the primary enemy of the Iranian peoples and the Islamic Republic of Iran"(44).

While Yeni Yol met all the Soviet requirements for publication, it apparently did not meet those of the Islamic Republic of Iran for it was closed down by Iranian authorities after less than a year of publication. A letter from a member of the Azerbaijan Culture Society which was published in Baku claimed that its closing was part of a trend in Iran:

> The Iranian revolution established a new life in Southern Azerbaijan and created the conditions for its all-round development. As a result, books, magazines and newspapers were published in the Azeri language. But the hands of reaction are still felt among us. Some magazines, including Yeni Yol, have been closed down. We hope for action by militant Azerbaijanis, poets and writers. We believe that sooner or later the activity of the American imperialists and their henchmen will be exposed(45).

By the beginning of 1984 all "progressive" Azeri publishing activity in Iran had come to a halt. Moscow and Baku viewed this crackdown as anti-Azeri, anti-national act, and this view was widely publicized in Soviet Azerbaijan. Mirza Ibrahimov wrote that

> recently bad news has come from Iran once again. Black clouds are gathering on the horizon, reaction has spread its wings, progressive forces are under fire, and

writers and poets who sing of patriotism,
even those composing lyric verse on the
love, truth and faithfulness of the human
heart are being persecuted.
Why?
Because they write in the mother tongue, in
Azeri!(46)

In fact, the Iranian moves against Azeri
publishing were more anti-Soviet than anti-Azeri.
And the Soviet efforts in Iranian Azerbaijan were
beginning to be countered by an increasing entrenched Muslim Iranian government.

NOTES

1. Azarbayjan Sovet Adabiyyaty Tarikhi, II
(Baku, 1967), p. 24.
2. Fedin is quoted by Rashid Guliyev in "Bir
roman barada ra'ylar", Azarbayjan, 10/1981, pp.
82-83.
3. Jafar Khandan, "Mirza Ibrahimovun Janub
Movzulary", Azarbayjan, 10/1981, p. 81.
4. Guliyev, op.cit., p. 83.
5. Azarbayjan Sovet Adabiyyaty Tarikhi,II,
p. 103.
6. ibid., p. 110; Ordubadi(1872-1950) had
covered the Constitutional movement in Iran as a
reporter for a number of Azeri newspapers and
periodicals prior to the Russian revolution and
had a firsthand acquaintance with developments in
Iran; he had died before the Russian translation
of Smoke-covered Tabriz was revised. The official
Azerbaijan Soviet Encyclopedia somewhat
inaccurately explains that the novel describes
the "national liberation struggle conducted by
the people of Southern Azerbaijan at the beginning of the XXth century". As explained in
Chapter One, there was no concept of national
liberation in Iranian Azerbaijan at that time;
the Constitutional movement was directed at
democratizing the Iranian government. cf.
Azarbayjan Sovet Ensiklopediyasy, VII (Baku,
1983), p. 369.

7. Azerbaydzhan SSR Akademiya Nauk. Rastsvet nauki Sovetskogo Azerbaydzhana (Baku, 1980), p. 315.

8. The only reference to this section appeared in Kommunist, 27 March 1983, p. 4 in an announcement that its chief scientific worker, Mirgasym Cheshmazer, had made an appearance at an Azerbaijan Writers Union discussion of the "Southern question". Another source identifies Cheshmazer as an "active participant in the national liberation, democratic movement of 1945-1946 in Southern Azerbaijan" and adds that he is now a scientific worker at the Institute of Oriental Studies of the AzSSR Academy of Sciences; cf. R. A. Seidov, "O natsional'nom formirovanii Azerbaydzhantsev v Irane", Voprosy natsional'no-osvoboditel'nogo dvizheniya na Blizhnem i Srednem Vostoke (Baku, 1985), p. 87 under footnote 37.

9. Abbas Zamanov, Adabiyyat va Injasanat, 7 March 1980, p. 6.

10. Latif Huseynov, chief editor of the Southern Desk of the Azerbayjan SSR State Television and Radio Committee, in Adabiyyat va Injasanat, 24 August 1984, p. 3.

11. Arif Ibrahimov, Adabiyyat va Injasanat, 4 February 1983, p. 7.

12. Azarbayjan dovri matbuaty, pp. 10, 123-124.

13. Mirza Ibrahimov, "Janubda dirchalish", Azarbayjan, 1/1980, p. 36; this article and a statement on the formation of an Azerbaijan Writers and Poets Association in Iran have been translated into English: cf. USSR Report: Baku Journal on National Liberation Literature from Iranian Azerbaijan (JPRS: 18 August 1980).

14. USSR Report contains good examples of anti-Shahist poetry emanating from Iran; cf. pp 14-26. A good example written by Balash Azeroghlu, an Iranian Azeri who emigrated to Soviet Azerbaijan in 1946, appears in the anthology Azerbaijanian Poetry(Moscow, 'Progress', 1969), pp. 409-415.

15. M. A. Yashar, "Azarbayjanda milli sitam haggynda", Varlyg (Tehran), 1/1979 is quoted by Ibrahimov, op.cit., p. 36.

62

16. "Azarbayjan Yazychylar va Shairlar
Jamiyyatinin ta'sisi ughrunda birinji ijlasda
gedan muzakiralar", Azarbayjan, 1/1980, pp. 58-
65.
17. ibid., p. 59.
18. ibid., pp. 59-60.
19. Noted by Ilhan Basgoz in "Varlyg: A New
Cultural Movement in Azerbaijan", Turkish Studies
Association Bulletin, II/3, p. 37.
20. Ibrahimov, op.cit., p. 39.
21. Bakhtiyar Vahabzade Adabiyyat va
Injasanat, 8 February 1980, p. 7.
22. Basgoz, op.cit., p. 36.
23. Bakhtiyar Vahabzade Adabiyyat va
Injasanat, 7 March 1980, p. 7.
24. Abbas Zamanov Adabiyyat va Injasanat, 7
March 1980, p. 7.
25. Balash Azaroghlu Adabiyyat va Injasanat,
4 November 1983, p. 6.
26. Hokuma Billuri Adabiyyat va Injasanat,
23 May 1980, p. 4; the response by the Iranian
Azeri poet Savalan appeared in Adabiyyat va
Injasanat, 25 July 1980, p. 7.
27. Ali Tuda Adabiyyat va Injasanat, 22
August 1980, p. 4 and Azerbayjan Muallimi, 27 May
1981, p. 4.
28. Ali Tuda Adabiyyat va Injasanat, 18 July
1980, p. 7.
29. Balash Azaroghlu Kommunist, 16 June
1981, p. 3; he was awarded the 'people's writer
of Azerbaijan' title on 13 May 1981.
30. Balash Azaroghlu, "Hijranly gunlarim
sirdashy", Azarbayjan, 7/1981, pp. 79-80.
31. Madina Gulgun Adabiyyat va Injasanat, 3
June 1983, p. 4.
32. Shamil Salmanov Adabiyyat va Injasanat,
19 June 1981, p. 6.
33. Mirza Ibrahimov, "Janub sovgaty",
Azarbayjan, 5/1981, pp. 6-7.
34. Hamid Mammadzade Adabiyyat va Injasanat,
18 September 1981, p. 7.
35. Sabir Amirov Adabiyyat va Injasanat, 3
June 1983, p 6; it is unclear when this department was founded.
36. Azaroghlu Adabiyyat va Injasanat, 31
August 1984, p. 6.

37. A recent example of this kind of evaluation is Sabir Amirov's article on the works of the young Iranian Azeri poet Eldar Mughanly whose poetry has been praised for its patriotism; he is described as one of the Southern Azeri "fedai[guerrilla] of the pen". Cf. Adabiyyat va Injasanat, 22 August 1986, p. 6.

38. Adabiyyat va Injasanat, 28 September 1984, p. 4.

39. Mirza Ibrahimov Adabiyyat va Injasanat, 19 November 1982, p. 7.

40. Adabiyyat va Injasanat, 23 April 1982, p. 7.

41. Volume I of the anthology was published in 1981; volume II in 1983. Pre-publication excerpts from volume II were given under the rubric "Sarhadsiz soz sarvatimiz", Azarbayjan, 5/1983, pp. 81-88. Volume III has not yet been published as of this writing.

42. Sohrab Tahir Adabiyyat va Injasanat, 14 May 1982, p. 3.

43. Huseyn Duzgun Yeni Yol, No. 1 quoted in Adabiyyat va Injasanat, 23 July 1982, p. 7.

44. Mammadrza Afiyat Adabiyyat va Injasanat, 3 December 1982, p. 7.

45. Quoted by Ramin Afiyat Talab Adabiyyat va Injasanat, 25 November 1983, p. 8.

46. Mirza Ibrahimov, "Dur, vagti-sahardir", Azarbayjan, 2/1984, p. 166.

5

The Impact of the Fall
of the Pahlavis

In the period following the ouster of the
Shah, Soviet contacts with Iranian Azerbaijan were
predicated on the use of the Azeri language as the
primary means of national communication and the
exploitation of the vast Soviet propaganda apparatus for the delivery of its message. To fulfill
this objective, Soviet Azeri "Southern question"
experts drew on experiences gained in working
with the Southern Azeri "progressive" intelligentsia during their occupation of Iran during
the early and mid 1940s and honed these to match
the situation in post-Pahlavi Iran. It is not by
chance that the jargon peculiar to the language
of Azeri national awareness which had been formulated some forty years earlier was taken in its
entirety and inserted into the context of the
1980s. This was transmitted to their conationals
in Iran by various means, including the radio,
the telephone the mails and personal contacts. At
first, the new Iranian revolutionary government
placed no obstacles between senders and receiv-
ers, but as the Khomeini regime began to suspect
that demands for Azeri national autonomy under
Tehran's protection were masking a call for a
united Azerbaijan under some sort of Soviet
hegemony, it began to take steps to frustrate the
Soviet efforts. But this did not occur until 1982:
the Soviets had the period from 1979 to 1981 to
establish themselves as the arbiters of the Azeri
national destiny. The success or failure of these
efforts will have to be judged by history.

The Iranian Azeri writers who first came
into contact with the Soviets in 1941 were heirs
to a classic literary tradition that traced its
origins to the XIIIth century. Poetry was its
primary mode of communication(1), and its genres
were identical to those employed in other Muslim
countries. Often, the only national element in
the poetry is the language itself. At the same
time, the Azeri Turks also possessed a rich folklore which was also expressed in poetic, especially epic forms. Efforts made by Soviet Azeri
literary ideologists from 1941-1946 were directed
at developing a common symbolic language of
literary communication between themselves and the
"progressive" Iranian Azeri writers whom they had
attracted to their cause. As a body of poetic
imagery on national liberation evolved, so did a
style of expression. The elaborate stylistics and
Muslim cadences of medieval poetry were abandoned
and a metrically simple, monothematic style took
its place. Then, as now, the titles of poems published in the "progressive" media of both Soviet
and Iranian Azerbaijan conveyed their entire
content; e.g., "Azerbaijan" and "Fatherland".
The result of this literary activity is, to a
great extent, artistic doggerel with a strong
political content that could not be misin-
terpreted on any level. Above all, the use of
these politically acceptable symbolic points of
reference enabled Soviet observers to measure the
extent of their influence.
    Many Iranian Azeri writers who had been
active during the Azerbaijan Democratic Republic
had continued to produce works up to the fall of
the Shah that remained faithful to guidelines
which had been set down by the literary ideologists of Vatan Yolunda . While these writers
had not been published in Iran, Soviet "Azer-
baijanologists" were aware of their activities
and, in 1979, contacts were re-established
between Soviet Azeri poets and their "progressive" counterparts in Iran. The Soviet Azeri
public was kept informed on the apparent deepen-
ing of these literary connections.
    Soviet poets devoted their works to
colleagues in Iran in the hopes of eliciting a
response. First broadcast over Radio Baku, these

would appear soon afterwards in the Soviet Azeri
media. Sometimes, a Soviet poet would contact a
writer in Iran over the telephone (direct telephonic communications between Iran and Baku,
impossible in the postwar years under the Pahlavi
dynasty, were restored in 1979). Bakhtiyar
Vahabzade, for example, dedicated a poem to the
Iranian Azeri poet Shahriyar that was based on a
telephone conversation they had in January 1981.
Entitled "We are the same age", it makes the
point that Vahabzade had been free to develop as
a writer in his own language in the Soviet Union,
whereas

> The Shah tyrannized you...
>   You were forgotten
> In your native country, in your fatherland.
> You could not even write in your native
>   tongue...(2)

The message in the poem, of course, was directed
more at the Soviet Azeri population than at
Shahriyar.

Soviet National Liberation Symbolism in Iranian Azeri Poetry

Soviet national liberation symbolism was
designed to evoke a sense of a common history,
tradition and customs shared by both the Azeris
of Iran and the Soviet Union. Jafar Khandan, who
laid the foundations for the use of these elements during his tenure as editor of Vatan
Yolunda during 1944-1945, quoted a classical
verse by the medieval poet Khagani to support his
position:

> My tears weep with longing for the
>   fatherland;
> I say 'fatherland' with every
>   word I say(3).

His implication was that the modern use of patriotic themes was actually the continuation of
an Azeri tradition begun some 800 years earlier.
One of the primary reasons for the stress on a
patriotic tradition was to reinforce an Azeri
national identity that allegedly had been eroded

by centuries of exposure to Persian culture. Of
equal importance was that the Soviets considered
these symbols to be "progressive" in the sense
that they set the Azeris, as a people, apart from
other peoples; i.e., they conveyed a meaning only
to other Azeris, both in Iran and Soviet Azerbaijan.

One technique that Soviet Azeri writers exported to Iran was the enumeration of a series of
historical and pseudo-historical personages from
Azeri history or mythology; such listings were
intended to stimulate the sense of a common
revolutionary bond. This category includes real
historical figures such as Sattarkhan and Sheykh
Khiyabani who are viewed, somewhat anachronist-
ically, as "national" figures. The formula for
using these personages was established by the
Soviet Azeri poet Suleyman Rustam in his poem "My
Tabriz" which appeared in Vatan Yolunda:

> Sattarkhan, the great national commander who
> With fiery heart and fiery tongue
> Defined freedom for the people.
> Come, turn not from his road, my Tabriz!(4)

According to a standard Soviet Azeri literary
history, in the lines cited above "S. Rustam
turned to the rich revolutionary traditions of
the people of Southern Azerbaijan and demon-
strated that the contemporary liberation
movement must be further developed on the basis
of these valuable historical traditions"(5).

Zeynep Pasha, a woman who allegedly led an
uprising against a granary during the Tabriz
famine of 1895, also makes regular appearances in
Iranian Azeri national liberation poetry, a tradition also begun in the 1940s(6). Whether she was
fictional or real does not matter -- she exemp-
lifies the will of the people. The Babeks, an
eighth century dynasty which "led the struggle of
the Azerbaijani people against Islam, Arab
slavery and feudal tyranny"(7) also figure prominently in "progressive" verse, acquiring in the
minds of readers a nationalistic hue which could
not otherwise be established through the study of
sources relating to their period.

While the recitation of the names of historical and quasi-historical names was aimed at sup-
plying the Iranian Azeri "progressive" intelligentsia with a common heritage and a revolutionary tradition, other, more abstract symbols were
introduced to give them a common cause in the
present. Of these, one of the most often found is
"dawn" which represents enlightenment, the consum-
mation of the national liberation struggle. "Sun"
and "red" are used in a similar context. For example, a line by Suleyman Rustam, "I see the dawn
has taken the color of your blood" was answered by
the Iranian Azeri poet Shahriyar who stressed the
need to shed blood for freedom(8). Shahriyar's response was not answered by Rustam, but by the Soviet poet Vahabzade, who pointed out that "the value
of freedom is blood...No one claimed freedom's
price had to be smeared with blood, but it is your
insurance for the dawn"(9). The emigre poet Tuda
equated "dawn" with his arrival in the Soviet
Union in 1946 in the line "I was a freezing
morning which you warmed with your dawn"(10).
    Characteristic of "progressive" responses to
the Soviet Azeri overture is the 1979 poem "There
Is A Road Going Towards the Dawn" by the Southern
Azeri poet Dr. Hamid Nitgi, a part of which says:

        Go, your home is distant, yet close.
        Grit your teeth, do not get lost, be calm.
        Hope from no one a remedy for your grief;
        We are no one, you and I.
        If we die or if we live, it's still a road.
        Give me your hand, perhaps we'll reach home.
        If I should fall, my friend, continue down
            the road.
        Don't stop, move on, cross the mountains.
        I know there's a road going towards
            the dawn.
        While you have the strength, do not tire,
            move on...(11)

Other national liberation keywords include "road"
which, of course, "goes towards the dawn",
"mountains", which represent obstacles to be overcome, and "Araz". One of the striking elements
in Azeri poetry of this genre is its extremely
limited vocabulary.

Generically, this type of literature is
called the "poetry of longing", and any manifestations of it unearthed in contemporary Iranian Azeri literature receive high praise from
Soviet Azeri literary critics. A collection of
poetry by the Iranian Azeri writer Mahzun (also
known as Mammadali Fakhraddin) entitled The
Sickness of Longing, which stresses the unity of
Soviet and Iranian Azerbaijan, was called a "gift
from the fatherland"(12) by one Soviet reviewer.
Poems that not only long for the unity of Azerbayjan, but also for the Soviet way of life are
also prominently featured in the Baku literary
press. More than one hundred stanzas of the
Iranian Azeri poet Sahand's "Araz" were reprinted
in the Azerbayjan SSR in 1982 because it refers
to the Soviet side of the Araz River as a "world
of labor, the hearth of socialism, a nest of
felicity"(13). Shahriyar's phrase "There was
Baku, our red Ka'ba"(14) is perhaps one of the
most frequently quoted lines from Iranian Azeri
poetry in the Soviet Union.
     When Iran's government began to close down
Azeri publications they considered to be pro-
Soviet, Soviet Azeris found it more difficult to
obtain feedback. Those writings which did manage
to reach Baku, however, still pleased Soviet
Iran-watchers. Balash Azaroghlu praised the
content ("the fatherland, freedom, the Araz,
revolution, etc.") of works he had received from
the South through the mail in August 1984(15)
and, by the summer of 1985 critics who had been
reviewing Iranian Azeri publications before the
Iranian crackdown began to concentrate on
"progressive" Iranian Azeri newspapers and
magazines published by the post-1979 emigration
from Iran(16).

Soviet Propaganda Organs and Iranian Azerbaijan
     Heydar Aliyev, then first secretary of the
Central Committee of the Communist Party of Azer-
baijan, stated in his 1981 address to the VIIth
Congress of Writers of Azerbaijan:

     Comrades! I want to touch on one question.
     Writers from Southern Azerbaijan are working
     productively as members of the republic

Writers Union. The leadership of the creative
union must always pay attention to them and
disseminate their works, both inside and
outside the republic. Generally, we must
think about strengthening literary relations
with Southern Azerbaijan, developing broad
contacts in all sectors of cultural and
intellectual creativity and imparting to our
comrades of the pen the rich esthetic-
artistic experience we have accumulated(17).

In the sense of "developing broad contacts"
with Iranian Azerbayjan, Radio Baku probably remains the most effective channel for the delivery
of Soviet propaganda to Iran. Broadcasts to Iranian Azerbaijan began in 1941. At present its
broadcasts fall into two categories: programs
designed to highlight achievements and advances
taking place in the Azerbaijan SSR "for Southern
Azeri, Persian, Turkish and Arabic-speaking
countries"(18), and programs based on positive
feedback from the target audience. The chief
editor of Radio Baku's Southern Azerbaijan Desk
has noted that "the new scope gained by the
literary movement in the South has exerted a
positive influence on the artistic content of our
programming". He added that a number of new programs had been added to the schedule as a result
of listener response and explained that "the
literary process going on in the South and the
works of writers living there make up the core of
these broadcasts. Separation, longing, love of
the fatherland, singing of the ideas of freedom
and calling the people to happiness constitute
the most important themes of the poems we
select"(19).
        Radio Baku uses a number of techniques to
elicit listener response. One of them, the poet-
to-poet approach, supplements and amplifies the
Writers Union technique wherein a Soviet Azeri
poet addresses a poem to his Iranian counterpart
in order to receive a "public" answer. Suleyman
Rustam, for example, broadcast a poem dedicated
to Shahriyar in 1979, and Shahriyar broadcast his
response over Radio Tabriz in the same year(20).
Other Soviet Azeri poets, writers and emigres
have done much the same.

Contests are another important means to stimulate audience response. A 1981 contest sponsored jointly by the Southern Azerbaijan and Iran Desks on the life and works of a classical Azeri-Persian poet reportedly received a number of responses from both Azeri and Persian listeners in Iran(21).

Listeners' letters are often quoted in the press: one listener wrote in to say that "you are destroying the border between North and South through your beautiful broadcasts"(22) and another expressed the hope that "friendly and fraternal relations between our two countries will be broadened"(23). The majority of these letters printed in the Baku press, however, concerned language. Characteristic of these is one which stated: "We listen to your broadcasts with great interest because they are in our native, sweet Azeri language"(24).

According to a letter from Tabriz, Radio Baku programs are also taped and recirculated in Iranian Azerbaijan(25); Balash Azaroghlu's speech at the VIIth Congress of Writers of Azerbaijan on the importance of Iranian Azerbaijan in Azeri culture was broadcast over Radio Baku, then taped in Tabriz and published in the Iranian Azeri literary magazine Dada Gorgut(26).

The Azerbaijan Society for Friendship and Cultural Relations with Foreign Countries is the foreign liaison arm of both the Communist Party of Azerbaijan and the Azerbaijan SSR government. One of its functions is to maintain contacts with Azerbaijanis abroad, including those in Iranian Azerbaijan. The Society coordinates its activities with those of the Azerbaijan Writers Union, other creative unions such as the Azerbaijan Journalists Union, the AzSSR Academy of Sciences and the AzSSR State Television and Radio Committee. These functions are under the supervision of the Foreign Relations Department of the Central Committee on the Communist Party of Azerbaijan. Its chairman is Nabi Khazri, a prominent poet who writes often on the "Southern question" and a candidate member of the Central Committee of the Azerbaijan Communist Party.

The Society publishes two magazines: Soviet Azerbaijan, which appears in Russian, English,

French, Arabic, Persian and Turkish and had a
circulation of 700 in 1981(27); and Odlar
Yurdu('Land of Fires'= Azerbaijan), a newspaper
directed at "compatriots abroad" that is published in Azeri in the modified Cyrillic, Latin
and, since 1982, Arabic scripts(28). The decision
to publish in Arabic script was clearly designed
to attract a greater readership among the Iranian
Azeris.

The Society was probably responsible for the
1982 visit of a group of Southern Azeri writers
to Baku in 1982 to mark the 60th anniversary of
the USSR and to participate in "literary meetings
connected to praising the USSR in Southern Azerbaijani literature"(29). It also distributes
books and other Soviet publications in Iran. A
"letter to the editor" from Iranian Azerbaijan
revealed that it arranged for book shipments and
newspaper subscriptions between Soviet and
Iranian Azerbaijan(30).

"One Azerbaijan"
The Soviet decision to shift the emphasis of
their propaganda from the passive "longing" to
the more active, and to the Iranian government,
more threatening "One Azerbaijan" approach was
almost inevitable. First, the idea that the Azeri
Turks shared two fatherlands, one in Iran and the
other in the Soviet Caucasus was both artistically cumbersome and politically ambiguous; and
second, the Soviet understanding of nationality
typically requires that peoples sharing a common
language, traditions, customs and history be
united. Consequently, it should have come as no
surprise when Soviet propaganda organs adopted
the slogan "One Azerbaijan" in 1982.

This change, which appeared to imply not
only a full-scale national liberation war in
northwestern Iran but even that the Soviet Union
might seize this territory, was actively
countered by Iranian authorities. Azeri newspapers and journals advocating any form of
national self-determination in Iran were closed
down and members of the Tudeh Party were sub-
jected to repressions, intimidated, imprisoned,
forced underground or into the swelling post-1979
Iranian emigration. Initially, Soviet media in

Azerbaijan interpreted these moves as a consequence of the Iran-Iraq war, then they treated
it as a result of the intrigues of international
imperialism, and finally they viewed it as the
failure of the Iranian revolution.

This change in the thrust of Soviet
propaganda tactics began to manifest itself in
1981 when Mirza Ibrahimov proposed the formation
of a "national front" among the Azeris of Iran
and the "One Azerbaijan" concept was floated in
Soviet Azeri media. On the policy level, these
developments were clearly intended to exert
Soviet leverage on the Iranian government. Yet a
change was also occurring among the Soviet Azeri
creative intelligentsia. In the early 1980s a
postwar generation of Soviet Azeri writers had
begun to emerge. Unlike those who had preceded
them -- those for whom the Second World War had
been a climacteric -- the younger writers had
had no direct contact with the Azeris of Iran
and, prior to the overthrow of the Shah, had
written little on the "Southern question". They
were, however, steeped in traditions molded by
such establishment figures as Mirza Ibrahimov and
Suleyman Rustam. In their works on Iranian Azerbaijan there was no reference to the duality of
the fatherland; Soviet and Iranian Azerbaijan
were viewed as a whole, a national unity.

Suleyman Rustam expressed his approval of
this approach in June 1982 when he remarked that
"the discussions going on in the pages of our
press about our One Azerbaijan and One literature
are an extremely joyous event"(31). His statement, which he made at a Writers Union meeting to
mark the 60th anniversary of the Soviet Union,
was affirmed by others present, including the
first secretary of the Azerbaijan Writers Union,
the chief editor of the Yazychy publishing house,
the chief editor of the Writers Union weekly
newspaper and the department head of the special
Writers Union department concerned with Southern
Azeri literature. This was, in fact, the first
time that the phrase "One Azerbaijan" had been
used in the Soviet mass media.

A year earlier, Mirza Ibrahimov, claiming
that there was a concerted effort by "ultra-
reactionary circles" to "sow discord among

progressive forces and the intelligentsia" in
Iran, argued that there was only one response to
this:

> Unity! Assembling all revolutionary forces,
> all progressive, open-minded individuals
> and, putting all conflicts of ideas to the
> side, gathering the entire people, all pro-
> gressive forces in one front in the name of
> the great goal -- the liberation and
> progress of the fatherland, the felicity and
> uplift of the people.(32)

Shortly after Ibrahimov's call for a
national front, the question of Soviet and
Iranian Azerbaijan's national unity was discussed
on the Baku stage in the historical drama
"Khurshidbanu Natavan", which opened in the Fall
of 1981. The play, ostensibly dealing with the
XIXth century poetess and daughter of the last
Khan of Garabagh, Natavan, is actually concerned
with the national unity of the two parts of
Azerbaijan. One critic, pointing out that she
often ponders the fate of "all Azerbaijan" on the
stage, wrote that she "does not accept the con-
cepts of 'Northern' and 'Southern' Azerbaijan but
considers it one Azerbaijan; she wishes to see
the fatherland, which had been divided into two
parts, as a whole"(33).

The new slogan was an immediate success. A
Soviet Azeri poet was able to figuratively stroll
along the north(Soviet) bank of the Araz River
and state that "this side is the fatherland, that
side the fatherland"(34) and another of the
"literary youth" repudiated the dual fatherland
hypothesis by demanding "May Azerbaijan not be
said twice!"(35).

A significant byproduct of the discussions
of the "Southern question was that it became a
channel for the expression of a Soviet Azeri
nationalism which could not be expressed in the
USSR. For example, the use of the word "fatherland": in conventional usage, statements such as
"if a talented poet or prose writer does not
write publicistic articles, then he is not
attached to the Fatherland or people"(36) or
"some youths...are not prepared to fulfill their

sacred obligations to the Fatherland" (37),
"fatherland" means the Soviet Union. In poetry
devoted to the "Southern question", however,
"fatherland" means Azerbaijan, as in Ali Tuda's
line "Where is the sorrow greater than the
Fatherland's" (38) which refers to the sorrow of
Azerbaijan because it is divided. Admittedly,
this style of expression is designed to be
exported into Iran but the fact remains that it
is primarily produced and consumed in Soviet
Azerbaijan where it cannot but help to vitiate
"Soviet patriotism."

In line with this new national ideology, the
literary critics also began to reevaluate the
work of the older generation. In a study of the
works of Suleyman Rustam devoted to the "Southern
question", one young critic pointed out that "the
indivisibility of the fatherland, the spiritual-
historical unity of the people and criticism of
the Iranian chauvinists' humiliation of the Azeri
people have constituted one of the major ideational motifs of these poems"(39). Yet, an examination of Rustam's works reveals no direct
reference to the "indivisibility of the fatherland"; he either addresses Iranian Azeris as in-
dividuals or collectively as "brothers and sis-
ters". Azerbaijan's national unity is only
implied. This retrospective reinterpretation
seeks to impose a dialectical process on the
resolution of the Azeri national question. Eyvaz
Borchaly, for example, is praised for "dialectical unity" in a poem in which he longs for
Tabriz; the reviewer pointed out that the poet
"passionately intervenes in one of the significant social issues of the time -- 'If the
Fatherland is one, why is my one Fatherland
divided?"(40). In this way, nationalistic long-
ings of Soviet Azeri poets for a united Azerbaijan give the illusion of satisfying ideological considerations.

The Araz River plays a major symbolic role
in any examination of a "Fatherland divided" for
it not only divides Azerbaijan, it also divides
villages and cities located along the riverbanks.
Julfa, in Soviet Azerbaijan, is located directly
across from Julfa in Iran. This has also led to
the expression of a kind of local nationalism in

Azeri poetry: the poem "Eynally-Eynaly" discusses
a village divided in such a manner. The poet,
addressing his "brother" in Iranian Azerbaijan,
states "I am here and you are there -- look at
our fate. We are separated from our one
village..."(41).

In the mid 1980s this physical division is
viewed symbolically as an unhealed wound in the
body of the fatherland. One critic, reviewing the
works of the poet Muzaffar Shukur (the author of
"Eynally-Eynaly" quoted above), pointed out that
his symbolic use of the Araz River "stirs our
feelings of longing and stimulates the desire for
the unity of the fatherland...It appears that the
passion of this separation, this longing, has
nested in the depths of his heart; without unification, this wound will not heal."(42)

While contemporary Soviet Azeri literature
has tended to stress the inevitability of unification, it does not claim that this is going to
occur in the immediate future. A recent collection of poetry by Bakhtiyar Vahabzade, for example,
said that this would occur "sooner or later"(43);
the emigre poet Balash Azeroghlu asserted in a
work entitled "Letter to the City of Tabriz"
that "if I do not see those days [of unification
with the South], my son will see them"(44). The
vagueness, even pessimism as to the imminence of
national unification was a reflection of political
reality. By 1982, even the most partisan onlooker
could see that Iran's Muslim regime had firmly
entrenched itself in the seat of power.

This setback to Soviet aspirations for
Iranian Azerbaijan had to be explained to the
Soviet Azeri population.

Iranian Azerbaijan and the "Failure of the Iranian Revolution"

Initial explanations appearing in the Soviet
Azeri mass media blamed the Iran-Iraq war for the
communication breakdown between Northern and
Southern Azerbaijan. Subsequently, Soviet analysts claimed that it was one facet of what came
to be referred to as the "failure of the Iranian
revolution".

The closing down of "progressive" Azeri
publications in Iran gave the Soviet public the

first evidence that a changing Iranian political
climate was impeding one of the immediate Soviet
goals, namely, the dissemination of the primary
attribute of Iranian Azeri national identity, the
language. At first, it was explained as a consequence of the Iran-Iraq war. As early as 1981,
Mirza Ibrahimov wrote that "this war, which
forces two neighboring countries to shed each
others' blood -- a necessity for none save
imperialists, shah-loving reactionaries and
Zionist terrorists -- has made the road to
achieve a number of goals and objectives of the
peoples of Iran more difficult"(45).

He concluded that these new difficulties had
engendered an atmosphere of pessimism throughout
Iran and Iranian Azerbaijan, and explained that
"under the present circumstances in Iran and
Southern Azerbaijan, the future of the struggle
against the powerful enemy appears clouded. And
this is not without reason. Although the workers
of Southern Azerbaijan have taken up arms three
times in the course of half a century and have
striven for victory under their brave sons
Sattarkhan, Sheykh Khiyabani and Pishevari, these
victories have been drowned in a sea of blood.
Along with those angered and inflamed by this and
ready to continue the struggle, there are also
those who face the future with hopeless
eyes"(46).

Initially, Soviet Iranists made an effort to
attribute the cause of the war to foreign manipulation rather than seeing it as one of the
results of the internal power struggle taking
place in Iran. An official of the Scientific
Information Center of the Azerbaijan SSR Academy
of Sciences stated that "facts reveal that the
Iran-Iraq war is in the interests of international imperialism" and added that "there is no
doubt that both warring parties understand the
goals of the imperialistic policy of the USA and
other Western countries...The conflict, now
having widened, has turned into an extended,
meaningless war"(47).

Yet the Soviets soon relegated the war to a
back seat behind the rising tide of Shi'ite
fundamentalism. For, in tandem with a resurgence
of the pan-Iranian ideology that denied the

existence of a nation of Azerbaijan, it was this
which effectively curtailed Soviet activities in
Iran.

By 1983 Soviet media began to intimate that
the Iranian revolution had failed, and blame was
placed on the "forces of the right", namely, the
Muslim clergy. As Soviet claims that the Shi'ite
mollas had assumed a reactionary role increased,
arguments based on the intrigues of "foreign
imperialists" in prolonging the Iran-Iraq war
were made less often. A year earlier, the Soviet
Azeri media had informed its readership that opposition to the Azerbaijani national cause in
Iran was being stimulated by imperialistic circles, meaning the United States. A letter written
to Radio Baku from Iran, for example, expressed
the idea that while the Iranian revolution "had
created a new life for Southern Azerbaijan and
the conditions for its multi-faceted development...the hands of reaction are still felt among
us" and added that "we believe that the activities of the American imperialists and their
henchmen will be exposed"(48). When the time came
to "expose" these imperialistic intrigues,
however, they were attributed instead to the
"forces of the right" within Iran.

In 1984 the chief editor of Radio Baku's
Southern Azerbaijan desk summed up the contents
of letters received from listeners in Iran and
reached the conclusion that "it is a regrettable
truth that the victorious people's revolution has
been unable to continue its advance due to the
perfidy of the forces of the right which have
taken over the government. Rights given to the
people by the dictates of the revolution have
been taken away step by step. National rights
promised to the people have come under the most
pressure and attack. Journals which had started
publishing were closed down. The publication of
enlightening books has been forbidden and poetry
has been burned"(49). A later Soviet Azeri
analysis of the situation in Iran highlighted an
additional concern: "In present-day Iran one
comes across many who attempt to inflame an anti-
Soviet mentality in a number of press organs and
propaganda channels. Chauvinist-bourgeois
"literary hooligans" are making an effort to

80

slander the economic achievements of the Soviet
Union, especially Soviet Azerbaijan, in their
writings, and creating a negative opinion about
our literature and fine arts; they are even
trying to propagate hostile ideas about Soviet-
Iranian relations"(50).

There were, of course, attempts to fix the
blame for these events on a conspiracy between
the Muslim clergy and foreign intelligence
agencies. When the Tudeh Party was banned in
1983, Mirza Ibrahimov proclaimed that "it is not
by chance that the infamous SAVAK and American
and Israeli intelligence agencies are involved in
the terror directed against Tudeh and other
progressive, freedom-loving intellectuals; they
have entered into a firm union with ultra-
reactionary, uneducated, ignorant fanatics and
the plundering, reactionary, wealthy classes who
have set Iran back a thousand years"(51).

Naturally, many in Iran who opposed what
they perceived as Soviet meddling in Iran's internal affairs, and Soviet scholarly works with a
less propagandistic bent isolated two factions
within Iran which opposed national rights for
Iranian Azerbaijan: certain factions within the
Muslim clergy and the still powerful pan-Iranian
ideologists. Soviet media concentrated its efforts on the latter, especially on those among
them who, Azeri by Soviet definition, considered
themselves to be cultural Persians. In this
connection, the Movgufat monograph series,
published in Tehran by Iranicized Azeris has come
under the most attack.

According to the theoretical monthly of the
Communist Party of Azerbaijan, the contents of
Movgufat consist of "scientific studies that are
complete slanders and falsifications of the
history of the people and language of Azerbaijan"(52). Furthermore, Soviet ideological
experts contend that the position taken by the
Movgufat group is identical to that of the
Shahist ideologues of Aryanism during the pre-
revolutionary epoch. To prove this, the introduction to a Movgufat monograph entitled The
Ancient Language of Azerbaijan is quoted as
saying "we must have one national language for
the national integrity and independence of Iran

and we will exploit all means to obtain this
goal"(53). The "one national language", of
course, is Persian.

Ad hominem arguments directed at members of
the Movgufat circle were also employed by Soviet
propagandists. The poet Bakhtiyar Vahabzade noted
in the introduction to a poem that "'scholars' in
Iran who deny the national existence of the Azerbaijani people and who cast aspersions on them
have emerged" and then proceeded to attack one
Yahya Zeka, an Iranicized Azeri and Movgufat
member for "betraying" his ancestors and
children(54).

When Movgufat began its activities in 1979,
Soviet influence in Iranian Azerbaijan was increasing and, because the Soviets had discounted
or disregarded its potential to disrupt their
efforts, it was not viewed as a threat to Soviet
interests. In Iranian Azerbaijan, however, this
was not the case; Yoldash, the major pro-Soviet,
Azeri literary magazine of the late 1970s and
early 1980s, often attacked members of this group
for their anti-national, or anti-Azeri lean-
ings(55). It is worthy of note that Soviet dia-
tribes directed against adherents of pan-Iranism
and against the "forces of the right" bore a
remarkable resemblance to those which had appeared in Soviet media during the reign of the
Shah.

Soviet Contact with the Post-1979 Iranian Azeri Emigration

Another pattern that recalled the Shah's
reign was the rise of a new Iranian emigration .
As had occurred earlier, the Soviets immediately
set out to establish contact with them. In
reports on these contacts, Soviet media hastened
to note that these people were not refugees from
Shahist tyranny, but rather from Khomeini's Iran.
Balash Azaroghlu, for example, described a meeting with three Iranian Azeri exiles "in one of
the old cities of Europe". Stressing that all
three had left Iran after the Iranian revolution,
he pointed out that "these youths will see that
the revolution dawns again"(56).

In an interview with an Iranian Azeri artist
living in Paris, the Soviet Azeri author Elchin,

paraphrasing Sheykh Khiyabani, noted that these
types of refugees are "the fedai [fighters] for
the future generation" and stressed that the new
emigre community is opposed to exploitation,
class inequality and national injustice(57). To
Soviet Azeris who were regularly reading these
report-ages, it must have been clear that Soviet
plans for Iran had received a major setback.

Later Soviet evaluations of their
achievements in Iranian Azerbaijan were mixed.
The most positive note was struck at a 1985
seminar on "Contemporary Southern Azeri literature and the struggle for freedom, democracy and
peace" which was jointly sponsored by the Azerbaijan Writers Union and the Nizami Institute of
Literature. The primary topic of discussion was
the relationship between literature and revolution since the February 1979 Iranian revolution.
They reached the conclusion that after the
revolution "a new stage began in the development
of Southern Azeri literature. Southern poets, for
whom the language had been forbidden for long
years, were liberated and they turned to new
themes: revolution, the fatherland, the mother
tongue, the Araz, sorrow, longing for unity and
respect for such heroes as Babek and Sattarkhan...poetry marched as one with the revolution.
[Under these circumstances] the ongoing literary
process in the south and north of Azerbaijan and
the literature created on both sides of the Araz
have become two native branches of our one,
contemporary Azeri literature"(58).

Almost a year later, the head of the
Azerbaijan Writers Union took a more pessimistic
tone: "Comrades, one of the major themes of our
literature, especially our poetry, is the longing, the craving for Southern Azerbaijan. This,
according to demand, sometimes surges forth and
sometimes stills. But we do not conceal it: our
wounds fester. We stare at the Araz; we spit out
our heartache and bitterness into the Araz" and
added that in Iran "reactionary forces have
strangled freedom and independence once
again"(59).

NOTES

1. Prose did not begin to develop as a
literary form in Iranian Azerbaijan until the
twentieth century and, due to restrictions placed
on the development and use of Azeri in Iran, it
never gained the prestige of poetry. It must be
added that, unlike the West, poetry remains a
primary channel of communication.
2. Bakhtiyar Vahabzade Adabiyyat va
Injasanat, 3 April 1981, p. 8.
3. Jafar Khandan, "Iran Azarbayjanynyn
vatanparvar shairlari", Azarbayjan(a), 1(6),
January 1946, p. 16.
4. Cited in M. Arif(ed.), Azarbayjan Sovet
Adabiyyaty Tarikhi,I (Baku, 1967), p. 481.
5. ibid..
6. Cf. Shishgilani, "Zeynep Pasha",
Azarbayjan(a), 7(12), July 1946, p. 32 and S.
Abufazl, "Zeynab Pasha haggynda ikinji sher",
Azarbayjan (a), 9(15), September 1946, p. 34.
7. "Babak harakati", Azarbayjan Sovet
Ensiklopediyasy,I, pp. 522-523.
8. Suleyman Rustam Azarbayjan, 4/1980, p 61.
9. Bakhtiyar Vahabzade Adabiyyat va
Injasanat, 7 March 1980, p. 7; the poem is
entitled "Answer to Master Shahriyar's Letter to
Suleyman Rustam."
10. Ali Tuda Adabiyyat va Injasanat, 22
August 1980, p. 4.
11. Cited in Azarbayjan, 1/1980, p. 38.
12. Sabir Amirov Adabiyyat va Injasanat, 1
January 1982, p 6.
13. Sahand Adabiyyat va Injasanat, 24
September 1982, p 7.
14. cf. Sohrab Tahir Adabiyyat va Injasanat,
11 December 1981, p. 7; the Ka'ba is the shrine at
Mecca towards which Muslims bow when praying.
15. Balash Azaroghlu Adabiyyat va Injasanat,
10 August 1984, p. 3.
16. A. Mammadrza Adabiyyat va Injasanat, 28
June 1985, p. 7.
17. Speech reported in Adabiyyat va
Injasanat, 19 June 1981, p. 2. It has been
suggested by Roy Medvedov that Aliyev's
involvement with Iranian Azerbaijan goes back to
the early postwar years when he "carried out

84

difficult assignments" there; cf. <u>Washington Post</u>, 16 December 1984. While it may be purely coincidental, it was during Aliyev's tenure as party chief in Azerbaijan that many of the organization concerned with Iranian Azeri questions in the AzSSR were established.

18. I. Rahimli <u>Kommunist</u>, 7 May 1982, p. 3.
19. Latif Huseynov <u>Adabiyyat va Injasanat</u>, 24 August 1984, p 3.
20. A transcription of Shahriyar's response to Rustam is given in <u>Adabiyyat va Injasanat</u>, 8 February 1980, p. 7.
21. Agshin Babayev <u>Adabiyyat va Injasanat</u>, 9 October 1981, p. 7.
22. Cited in <u>Adabiyyat va Injasanat</u>, 13 November 1981, p. 8.
23. Cited by Arif Ibrahimov <u>Adabiyyat va Injasanat</u>, 3 December 1982, p. 7.
24. Cited by Arif Ibrahimov <u>Adabiyyat va Injasanat</u>, 4 February 1983, p. 7.
25. Cited in <u>Adabiyyat va Injasanat</u>, 13 November 1981, p. 8.
26. Abbas Zamanov <u>Adabiyyat va Injasanat</u>, 13 November 1981, p. 8.
27. <u>Kommunist</u>, 14 October 1981, p. 4.
28. <u>Kommunist</u>, 29 January 1982, p. 4.
29. <u>Adabiyyat va Injasanat</u>, 13 November 1982, p. 5.
30. <u>Adabiyyat va Injasanat</u>, 29 April 1983, p. 8.
31. <u>Adabiyyat va Injasanat</u>, 4 June 1982, p.6.
32. Mirza Ibrahimov, "Janub Sovghaty", <u>Azarbayjan</u>, 5/1981, p. 8.
33. Abbas Zamanov <u>Kommunist</u>, 4 October 1981, p 4. Khurshidbanu Natavan was an important historical and cultural figure of XIXth century Azerbaijan. She was the daughter of the last Khan of Garabagh and a poetess reknowned for her elegiac works. Her nom-de-plume Natavan is from the Persian and means "powerless, impotent". Her poetry has only recently gained party approval; as late as the mid 1960s an official history of Azerbaijan found that "despite a number of positive characteristics in Natavan's poetic legacy, she was unable to relate her creative work to the life of the people or the demands of

85

the time"[Azarbayjan Tarikhi,II, p 408]. Despite
party disapproval of her artistic output, the
club attached to the Azerbaijan Writers Union was
named after her in 1946. From that time to the
present, the club has remained one of the primary
forums for the discussion of the "Southern
question"; hence, it is unsurprising that her
name has been connected with the cause of
Southern Azeri national unity. Historically,
there is no evidence of any such relationship.
Ilyas Afandiyev's play "Khurshid Banu Natavan",
which contains allusions to the unity of
Azerbaijan in almost every scene, was published
in Azarbayjan, 11/1985, pp. 22-65.

34. Gasham Ilgar Azarbayjan, 7/1981, p. 148.
35. Hasan Valeh Azarbayjan, 9/1981, pp. 110-
111.
36. Sayavush Sarkhanly Kommunist, 4 May
1986, p. 3.
37. UzTAG.Sovet Turkmenistany, 17 May 1986,
p. 3. In both this instance and the one cited in
footnote 36, appeals are made to Soviet patriotism.
38. Ali Tuda Adabiyyat va Injasanat, 11 July
1986, p. 4.
39. Isfandiyar Vahabzade, "Mubariza
illarinin tarannumu (S. Rustam janub poemalary)",
Azarbayjan, 12/1983, p. 175.
40. Elchin Adabiyyat va Injasanat, 2 March
1984, p. 6.
41. Muzaffar Shukur Azarbayjan, 6/1984, p.
85.
42. Elchin Adabiyyat va Injasanat, 14
December 1984, p. 6.
43. Cited by Yusif Seyidov in Kommunist, 22
January 1983, p. 4.
44. Balash Azaroghlu Adabiyyat va Injasanat,
22 June 1984, p. 8.
45. Mirza Ibrahimov, "Janub Sovghaty",
Azarbayjan, 5/1981, p. 10.
46. ibid., p. 14.
47. Javanshir Afandiyev Kommunist, 26 June
1984, p. 3.
48. Arif Ibrahimov, quoting a letter from
Ramin Afiyat Talab, a member of the Azerbaijan
Culture Society in Iran, Adabiyyat va Injasanat,
25 November 1983, p 8.

49. Latif Huseynzade Adabiyyat va Injasanat, 24 August 1984, p. 3.

50. Rovshan Aliyev Adabiyyat va Injasanat, 9 August 1985, p. 2.

51. Mirza Ibrahimov, "Dur, vagti-sahardir", Azarbayjan, 2/1984, p. 167.

52. V. Gukasyan and A. Tagirzade, "Fal'sifikatsiya v izyashchnoy oblozhke", Kommunist Azerbaydzhana, 11/1984, p. 91.

53. ibid., p. 92.

54. Bakhtiyar Vahabzade Adabiyyat va Injasanat, 17 February 1984, p. 8.

55. Yoldash, No.4(1979) quoted in Azarbayjan, 1/1980, pp. 55-58.

56. Azaroghlu Adabiyyat va Injasanat, 6 April 1984, p. 8.

57. Elchin Adabiyyat va Injasanat, 6 January 1984, p. 5.

58. Adabiyyat va Injasanat, 12 July 1985, p. 7. The report also lists a number of Southern Azeri modern writers who are considered "patriotic poets of Azerbaijan": Sonmaz, Huseyn Duzgun, Alakbar Haddad, Rza Barahani, Hamid Nitgi, Ali Tabrizi, Gaflanty, Turkoghlu, Suleyman Salis, Chayoghlu, Abbas Farig, Firidun Hasarly, Bahman Zamani, Aziz Salami, Aziz Mahsini, Gulamrza Majdfar, Adsyz, Valeh, Aydyn, Marziya Uskuyi, Alirza Nabdil, Hamid Seyidnagavi, Alov, Abbas Sabiri, Gahraman Khatibi, Huseynali Shagagi.

59. Speech by Ismayyl Shykhly. Adabiyyat va Injasanat, 30 May 1986, pp. 2-4.

6

The Current Soviet-Iranian Competition for Iranian Azerbaijan

Introduction
        Of the three countries on the Soviet border
which are not now under Soviet influence -- Iran,
Turkey and the Peoples Republic of China -- Iran
is easily the most susceptible to Soviet penetration. Under these circumstances the Soviet approach to Iranian Azerbaijan, its successes and
failures from 1979 to the present, deserves
special scrutiny.
        The Soviet manipulation of the Azerbaijanis
of Iran met with undeniable success during the period 1979-1981. An immediate consequence was a hard-
ening of anti-Soviet attitudes within the Iranian
government and increasing efforts to stem the demands of ethnic movements for local autonomy. Soviet aspirations for the region were voiced in Azeri
Marxist-Leninist opinion magazines published in
Tehran and Tabriz, and ideas which they generated
were echoed in the numerous literary journals
which advocated linguistic and cultural autonomy
for minorities within Iran. Personal, epistolary
and telephonic contacts were initiated between
the Soviet Azeri intelligentsia and their counterparts in the South. Radio Baku broadcasts directed
at the Iranian Azeri listening audience were well
received, and transcripts of especially effective
programs found wide circulation among the population and were reprinted often in both the Southern and Soviet Azerbaijani media. During this period Soviet influence in Iran was at its greatest
height since the Soviet occupation in 1941-1946.

As Soviet-Iranian relations began to
deteriorate from 1981 onward, so did the overt
manifestations of Azerbaijani nationalism in
Iran. This may be directly linked with the increasing isolation of the Tudeh Party which,
having initially supported the Khomeini regime,
came to find itself ouside the mainstream of the
Islamization of Iran. By June 1981 its newspaper
was closed down; in 1983 Tudeh itself was banned
and its leadership arrested. One can only assume
that the loosely-knit "national front" of "progressive" Azerbaijani nationalists and commun-
ists who were able to escape the mounting repressions directed against them by the Muslim clerg-
ical apparatus went underground and will emerge
only when the struggle for Khomeini's successor
begins.

The careful mobilization of the Soviet Azeri
media and other state organs around the Southern
Azerbaijani cause is impressive. A chronological
examination of the content of this Soviet literature reveals a sophisticated orchestration and
manipulation of terminology, the primary example
of which is the sudden shift from the Soviet
Azerbaijani "longing" for their brethren in the
South to the all-embracing concept of "One Azerbaijan" in 1981. This also reveals the tactical
flexibility inherent in Soviet political-
propagandistic formulations: they are able, for
example, to declare the Iranian Azeri Turks to be
part of the same nation as the Soviet Azeri Turks
despite the inability of Marxist-Leninist
theoreticians to make a clear distinction between
a "nation", an "ethnosocial community" and a
"people". This reveals the real Soviet intentions
for the region since Soviet nationality theory is
always subordinate to Soviet foreign policy
objectives.

The Development of the Modern Soviet Approach to Iranian Azerbaijan

There have been two different Soviet approaches to Iranian Azerbaijan during the
century. The first phase, in which one would
include pre-Soviet Bolshevik attempts to create a
revolutionary situation in northwestern Iran,
began in 1905 and continued until the collapse of

the Gilan Soviet Republic in the early 1920s: it was characterized by a mixture of revolutionary zeal and a total ignorance of local Iranian conditions, the most important of which being the devotion of the local populations -- Azeri and Iranian -- to Islam. Evidence of this was the strength of the Khiyabani movement in the face of Bolshevik efforts to undermine it. Although Bolshevism did acquire a small foothold in Iranian Azerbaijan through the efforts of Azeri cadres trained in pre-World War One Baku, the growing strength and political awareness of the Iranian government and its supporters were easily enough to overcome these half-hearted Soviet ventures. A second factor was that nationalism had not yet taken root in Iran, nor did Soviet ideologists feel that it could be developed and exploited in the Soviet interest until the mid 1940s.

The Soviet decision to make use of its own Azerbaijani cadres in establishing contacts with the Iranian Azeri population marked the beginning of the second phase of the Soviet approach. This phase, which endures to the present, is characterized by an increasing Soviet sophistication in the study and analysis of local Iranian conditions. At the same time, a post-Stalin shift in Soviet internal policy allowed a greater latitude in expressions of national awareness in the Soviet Union itself. As a result, it became possible to exploit the Soviet Azerbaijanis to advocate the national liberation of Iranian Azerbaijan and, ultimately, to use them as bannerbearers of a "One Azerbaijan". This greater permissiveness granted to expressions of national awareness in the Azerbaijan SSR can be clearly seen in the examination of Soviet Azeri institutions concerned with the "Southern question".

The process of the institutionalization of the "Southern question" in the Soviet Union began in 1941 when Soviet Azeri political advisors arrived in Tabriz in the wake of the Red Army. The first significant development in this process was the publication by them of the Tabriz political-literary newspaper Vatan Yolunda which became the first instance of Soviet and Iranian Azeri collaboration since the Russian Revolution. Fol-

lowing the establishment of the Azerbaijan Democratic Republic in 1945, the bi-monthy magazine
Azarbayjan, published by the Soviets in the
Arabic script, continued this collaboration. With
the withdrawal of the Red Army from Iran and the
subsequent collapse of the Azerbaijan Democratic
Republic, these institutional developments came
to an end. Their primary significance lay in the
fact that many of the personnel involved in these
joint ventures, both Soviet and Iranian, came to
play leading roles in promoting the national
liberation of Iranian Azerbaijan in later years.

With the exception of literary activity
generated by Soviet Azeris who had served in
Iranian Azerbaijan and that of their Iranian
Azeri colleagues who had taken refuge in the
Azerbaijan SSR, the question of the national
liberation of Iranian Azerbaijan received little
attention from other sectors of society until
1955. Then, the USSR Academy of Sciences decreed
that a "major center" be established in Baku for
the study of modern Iran in Baku; it is now a
part of the Institute for the Study of the
Peoples of the Near and Middle East. Its priorities include the examination of ways and means
to foment national liberation and revolutionary
movements in a Muslim context. In retrospect,
this was a significant step in attracting a wider
segment of the Azeri intellectual, academic and
political community into the consideration of the
"Southern question". The decision to create this
center had been preceded by two developments:
first, the outpouring of literary works advocating the national liberation of Iranian Azerbaijan which had appearedd between 1948 and 1955;
and second, the overthrow of Iran's Prime
Minister Mossadegh and the return of the Shah to
Iran from his exile in Rome -- perhaps the most
serious blow to Soviet plans for Iran since the
end of World War Two. It is worthy of note that
for twenty years following the establishment of
this center, not one overt move was made to
publicize the national cause of Iranian Azerbaijan in the Soviet mass media.

Between 1955 and 1976 Soviet analysts were
trying to develop more effective techniques to
deal with Iran and Iranian Azerbaijan. The most

important decision made during this period was to
give national differences a greater emphasis than
class differences. This move had two consequences
in Soviet Azerbaijan: first, it directly affirmed
the national legitimacy of Soviet Azerbaijan and
indirectly justified Marxist-Leninist principles
of nation-building; second, it gave the mandate
to Soviet Azerbaijani institutions to transmit
this legitimacy to their conationals in Iranian
Azerbaijan. In other words, it laid the foundations for an Azerbaijani irredentist movement
sponsored by the Soviet state.

Soviet Azerbaijani institutions devoted to
various facets of the "Southern question" began
to proliferate in 1976 with the formation of the
Section for Southern Azerbaijani Language and
Literature under the Nizami Institute of Literature of the Azerbaijan SSR Academy of Sciences.
This type of institutional development gained
impetus with the ouster of the Shah in late 1978.
At present, departments concerned solely with
this question have been established under the
auspices of the Azerbaijan Writers Union and its
weekly newspaper Adabiyyat va Injasanat, the
Ministry of Education and its newspaper
Azarbayjan Muallimi, the Faculty of Journalism at
the S. M. Kirov Azerbaijan State University, the
Azerbaijan Society for Friendship and Cultural
Relations with Foreign Countries, and Radio Baku.
Since 1979 Soviet Azeri media have been able to
keep their interpretations of the past, present
and future of the Azeri Turks of Iran constantly
in the public eye.

The articles and other writings appearing in
the media have both defensive and offensive
objectives: defensively, they seek to enhance the
image of the Soviet system of government with
regard to its ability to assure national rights
to those fortunate enough to be its citizens;
offensively, they assert the superiority of
Soviet secular national rights over Muslim
theocracy in order to eliminate or reduce the
influence of Iranian propaganda aimed at the
Soviet Muslim population.

Soviet Nationality Theory and Iranian Azerbaijan

One element underplayed in contemporary Soviet writings on Iranian Azerbaijan is the relevance of Soviet nationality theory to the present situation: namely, are the Azeris of Iran genuinely part of a nation of Azerbaijan or not? The Soviet approach to this issue is both ambiguous and ill-defined.

Language, territory and a community of economic ties constitute the objective bases for nationhood and national self-awareness in modern Marxist-Leninist thinking. Some, but not all Soviet scholars would add a common ethnos to this. When one takes just these factors into consideration, it is clear that there is no "One Azerbaijan". Yet, it should be noted that if two very similar peoples are separated only by a political border, the objective situation could change very rapidly through either the application of force or diplomatic measures by one or both of the host states.

The strongest point in the Soviet argument for the common nationhood of Iranian and Soviet Azerbaijan is that they both speak the same language, and have spoken this same language for centuries. In this context, the contention of Persian scholars and ideologists that Azeris are actually Iranian peoples who had been 'turkified' during the Mongol invasions is irrelevant: the process of ethnolinguistic consolidation which occurred between the IXth-XIIth centuries created the community of Azeri Turks we find today.

Traditionally, Marxism-Leninism has held that a "nation" must go through certain evolutionary steps in its development. Beginning as a "tribe" in some distant past, it then coalesces into a "people" and, with the operation of both "objective" and "subjective" factors affecting the people collectively, it then forms itself into a people. Accompanying the people's emergence into nationhood is national awareness. In contemporary Marxist-Leninist national philosophy this is defined in the following manner:

> National awareness grows out of the same
> conditions which play a decisive role in the
> origin and development of a nation. A com-

> munity of economic ties, territory and
> language as well as a community of ethnic
> and national characteristics of psychology,
> culture, customs and traditions beget among
> representatives of the given nation an
> awareness of their national community --
> national awareness.(1)

Omitted in Soviet discussions is that a Soviet
"nation" lacks the authority to determine its own
destiny. According to the Marxist school of
thought, a "nation", like those evolutionary
steps which precede its formation, is a tran-
sitional state on the path to a world-wide
political, economic and social community of
mankind. In other words, national destiny is pre-
determined by the dialectical process.

   If a people share some, but not all of the
above-mentioned attributes, they may not be a
nation at all; they are, instead, an "ethnosocial
community". In modern Soviet sociology an "ethnosocial community" is only a synonym for the older
expression "people".(2)

   An ethnolinguistic map devoid of political
markers would demonstrate that the Azeri Turks of
Iran and the Soviet Union occupy a common territory. Politically, this means that one-third of
Azerbaijan is in the Soviet Union and the rest in
Iran. The promotion of the "One Azerbaijan"
school of Soviet literature over Radio Baku
programs directed into Iranian Azerbaijan is an
attempt to build a climate of opinion in the
South favoring national consolidation with their
ethnolinguistic brethren to the North. Even
taking current political realities into consideration, if the two Azerbaijans do not, in
fact, share a common territory, they do share
territorial contiguity which is one of the most
important conditions for national consol-
idation(3).

   The ambiguity in the Soviet approach lies in
the fact that neither the meaning nor the consequences of a people sharing a common ethnos
have been resolved in modern Soviet political
literature. The same author who stressed the need
for territorial contiguity as a precondition for
national consolidation also pointed out that "an

ethnic relationship is not a required condition
for the organization of a nation"(4). If there is
an ambiguity of interpretation associated with
the term "ethnic", there is even more concerning
the word "national". The rector of the Baku
Higher Party School noted that the term
"national" "not only expresses the internal
history of a given people, but also their ties
and relationships with other peoples" and then
pointed out that "a unity of economic and social-
political life constitutes the objective basis"
of this national process(5). Under these vague
and conflicting definitions Iranian Azerbaijan
could be considered a part of Iran just as easily
as part of a "One Azerbaijan" in current Marxist
thinking. In the final analysis, this would de-
pend on the "subjective factors" underlying the
formation of a nation.

Soviet propaganda directed at Iranian
Azerbaijan, both in its printed matter circulated
within Iran and Radio Baku's Southern program,
has been making a major effort to instill in the
minds of the Iranian Azeris those subjective
factors which would precondition them to accept
themselves as part of a Greater Azerbaijan. This
process requires the manipulation of ethnopsychological factors, many of which remain
undefined in contemporary Soviet writing on the
nationality question, although the great
"practical importance" of these factors was
recently stressed by a leading Soviet ethno-
psychologist(6). It is for this reason that
artists, primarily writers, have been used as
carriers of a subjective national awareness
because it is felt that the cultural similarities
in the literary process awaken a national
response in both Soviet and Iranian Azerbaijan.

In general, modern Soviet nationality
experts believe that a community of ethnic and
national psychological traits, as well as a
perceived common culture, customs and traditions,
underlie national awareness. Among these, the
ethnopsychological factors are deemed to be the
most important because "man's mentality is
begotten in his activity as both subject and
object"(7) -- man makes the society which, in
turn, makes the man. Considered collectively,

"the national-psychological characteristics of a
people...are formed and developed historically
and change together with changes in society as a
whole"(8).

Fundamentally, the issue revolves around to
extent to which Soviet Azeri society differs from
the Muslim Azeri society in Iran. Some Soviet
nationality theorists believe that the differences are superficial: Bromley, one of the leading Soviet ethnologists, feels that the people
themselves are "spontaneous carriers of the
national", but points out that national manifestations are a process and must be treated as
such. He adds, however, that "a decisive turning
point is needed in our social sciences in the
direction of a much deeper study of the real contents of national processes in all their com-
plexity and contradictions"(9). In brief, Soviet
propaganda directed at stimulating national
awareness among the Azeris of Iran is conducted
purely on an ad hoc basis and is apparently
guided not by Marxist-Leninist principles but
rather by Soviet foreign and internal policy
considerations.

Culture and Islam

Two of the most important obstacles to the
extension of Soviet influence in Iranian Azerbaijan are Persian culture and Islam. For
centuries Persian culture, primarily in literature and the arts, held sway over the Azeris,
and much of the common heritage they share today
finds its roots in Iran. Nizami of Ganja, considered the founder of classical poetry in
Azerbaijan in the XIIIth century, wrote all his
known works in Persian although he was Azeri
himself. While the Azeri Turkic elements in this
culture can easily be isolated, the point is that
it is language that distinguishes the two
peoples, not culture. Hence, the Soviet emphasis
on language to heighten differences between Azeri
and Persian.

Persification policies instituted among the
minorities of Iran since the end of World War Two
undoubtedly enhanced the appeal of Soviet propaganda advocating national-cultural autonomy for
the Iranian Azeris, not only among "progressives"

but also among nationalists and pan-Turkists. It
was to capitalize on this separatist sentiment
that Mirza Ibrahimov called for a national front,
an initiative which was only stymied when the
Muslim clergy solidified their control over the
Iranian government.

Islam is religion and way of life not only
in Iran but also in many parts of the Caucasus
and Central Asia. In Soviet propaganda directed
at Iranian Azerbaijan, Islam is dealt with by
omission: the centuries of cultural continuity
shared by the Azeris of both sides of the border
are represented in Soviet media by a common folklore and folk heroes embodying positive (i.e.,
non-Islamic, non-reactionary) attributes. During
the apogee of Soviet ideational influence in Iran
between 1979-1981 only occasional, neutral reference was made to Islam as one of many elements in
Iranian life. Subsequently, the tone of Soviet
media took on a hostile, anti-clergical emphasis.
Evidently, Soviet analysts were surprised by the
durative quality of the Khomeini regime, its
messianic zeal, its anti-Soviet stance and its
efforts to use Islam to counter the effects of
Soviet propaganda.

Iran's efforts to export its view of Islam
into the Soviet Union's Muslim borderlands are
resulting in an ideological confrontation within
the Soviet Union itself, especially in the Azerbaijan SSR. Official Soviet Shi'ism is represented
by the Sheykhulislam Allahshukur Pashazade (b.1949),
who heads the Spiritual Administration of the Muslims of the Transcaucasus in Baku and who studied
in Qum under the Ayatollah Shariat-madari. In
addition to the legal mosques and state-certified
clergy in Azerbaijan, editorials in the daily
newspaper of the Communist Party of Azerbaijan
have noted the existence of a number of
unregistered sectarian groups, illegal clergy and
shrines, and have criticized their existence(10).
A recent Western examination of Islam along the
Soviet-Iranian border concluded that "evidence
from recent editions of the native language media
in Azerbaijan and Turkmenistan points to the
Islamic Republic of Iran as being both directly
and indirectly responsible for stimulating Islam
and Islamic movements in these regions"(11).

The effect of the Iranian propaganda assault
on Soviet Azerbaijan has not gone unrecognized in
the Soviet Union. A lead editorial in the Baku
Communist Party daily attacking the activities of
unnamed "diversionary radio stations" noted that
their broadcasts "have stepped up even further in
connection with events taking place in Iran"(12).
The impact of the Islamic Revolution is being
felt most strongly in the Nakhchyvan ASSR, which
is situated directly across the Araz River from
Iranian Azerbaijan. A high-ranking Communist
Party official in Nakhchyvan, mentioning efforts
by "bourgeois ideologists...to strike out at the
friendship of peoples and national relations",
has pointed out that "party committees, taking
into consideration their location in the border
zone of the autonomous republic...are paying
special attention to counterpropaganda
questions"(13).

Religion has always been a major stumbling
block in Soviet efforts to indoctrinate their own
population with a Marxist-Leninist worldview. In
Muslim areas the problem is even more complex
because believers in Islam consider it to be an
important aspect of their own national awareness.
In the 1940s Moscow made a bureaucratic compromise with Islam and permitted the formation of
four Muslim directorates to administer and
regulate the affairs of Muslim believers in the
Transcaucasus, the North Caucasus, the Volga-Ural
region and Central Asia. Yet, the persistence of
illegal, or unauthorized Muslim clergy, shrines
and and rituals -- the fast of Ramazan, the
Shi'ite observance of Muharram, bride price -- is
well documented in Soviet sources. In the past,
Moscow's aspirations for Iran have run into the
same barrier of belief: Bolsheviks were unable to
undermine Sheykh Khiyabani's Azerbaijan Democratic Party in 1920 and efforts to establish a
Soviet republic in Gilan were no more successful.
Where the Soviet ideological apparatus has
reached both a compromise with Islam and with
local nationalism, as was the case in the formation of the Azerbaijan Democratic Republic,
Soviet goals have come closer to fulfillment.
Even this partial success was only achieved with
the protection of the Red Army.

In 1979 Soviet propagandists launched a
major effort to convince Iranian Azeris that the
national question is central to Iranian Azerbaijan's destiny. They clearly failed to foresee
the potential consequences that a government
composed of Shi'ite clergy would have on Soviet
aspirations for the region. Yet, in the eyes of
Moscow's policy makers, any setbacks they have
received are only temporary. They have succeeded
in establishing a fulcrum with which they hope to
exert a decisive influence over Iranian Azerbaijan's future, they have created over the last
several years a bureaucracy, or series of
bureaucracies, in the Azerbaijan SSR concerned
only with the "Southern question", and they have
undoubtedly acquired adherents within Iran
itself. Throughout this century, however, the
belief of the Azeris of Iran in Allah and Shi'ism
has thwarted any attempts by outsiders to impose
on them an alien ideology at the cost of
religion. Without the use of military force, it
is difficult to foresee the Soviet Union attaining their aspirations for Iranian Azerbaijan in
the near future

NOTES

1. S. T. Kaltakhchyan. <u>Marksistko-Leninskaya</u>
<u>teoriya natsii i sovremennost'</u>. (Moscow, 1983),
p. 189.
2. This question is discussed in detail in
Yu. V. Bromley's <u>Ocherk teorii etnosa</u>. (Moscow,
1983) and also stressed in the same author's
"Natsional'nyye aspekty dukhovnoy zhizni
cheloveka v istoricheskoy perspektive" in
<u>Aktual'nyye problemy natsional'nogo i</u>
<u>internatsional'nogo v dukhovnom mire sovetskogo</u>
<u>cheloveka</u>, vypusk 1, p. 30: the latter book cited
was compiled based on reports delivered at the
plenary meeting of the All-Union Scientific-
Practical Conference on the "Dialectic of the
National and International in the Spiritual Life
of Soviet Man", Baku, 6-9 September 1983.

3. Kaltakhchyan, op.cit., p. 190; he adds
that "nearness of culture and psychology", among
other factors, are equally important conditions.

4. ibid., p. 189.

5. F. K. Kocharli, "Rastsvet dukhovnoy
zhizni i natsional'noy kul'tury Azerbaydzhanskogo
naroda", Razvitiye natsii i natsional'nykh
otnoshenii v usloviyakh razvitogo sotsializma:
Materialy vyezdnogo zasedaniya Byuro Otdeleniya
Filosofii i Prava AN SSSR. (Baku, 1983), pp. 136-
137.

6. cf. B. F. Lomov, "Rol' psikhologicheskoy
nauki v razvitom sotsialisticheskom obshchestve",
Razvitiye natsii..., p. 156.

7. Kaltakhchyan, op.cit., p. 128 and
Kocharli, op.cit., p. 133.

8. Lomov, op.cit., p. 156.

10. cf. KommunistBaku), 23 March 1982, p 1.

11. David Nissman, "Iran and Soviet Islam:
The Azerbaijan and Turkmenistan SSRs", Central
Asian Survey, II/4(1983), p. 58.

12. Kommunist(Baku), 19 February 1985, p. 2.

13. D. Alakbarova, secretary of the
Nakhchyvan Obkom, 15 March 1985, p. 2.

Appendix A

1828   Treaty of Turkmanchay cedes Azerbaijan
            north of the Araz to Russia

1880-1914   Intensive industrialization of Baku

1904   Hummat, an Azerbaijani socialist study
            group, formed in Baku

1905   Hummat merges with the Russian Social
            Democratic Workers Party as an auto-
            nomous organization

1906   Ijtimaiyyun-Amiyyun, a political organ-
            ization of workers from Iran, organized
            in Baku under the auspices of Hummat

1908-1911   Sattarkhan leads constitutional rebel-
            lion in Tabriz

1916   Adalet organized as successor to
            Ijtimaiyyun-Amiyyun

1917   Russian Revolution

1918   Musavat Party declares Azerbaijan's
            independence

1920   Soviet government established in Baku

1920   Adalet merges with Communist Party of
            Iran

1920	Soviet fleet lands in Rasht and a delegation meets with Mirza Kuchuk Khan
1920	Mirza Kuchuk Khan declares formation of the Gilan Soviet Republic
1920	Sheykh Khiyabani announces government of Azadistan in Tabriz
1920	Communist Party of Iran ousts Mirza Kuchuk Khan from Gilan government
1920	Sheykh Khiyabani executed by Iranian government
1921	Soviet-Iranian Treaty signed
1921	Gilan abandoned by Soviets
1931	Communist Party of Iran banned by Iranian government
1941	Red Army occupies northern Iran
1941	Radio Baku begins regular broadcasts to Iran
1942	Vatan Yolunda, first joint Soviet-Iranian Azeri publication, organized under Red Army
1945	Formation of Azerbaijan Democratic Party in Tabriz
1945	Azerbaijan provincial organization of Tudeh merges with Azerbaijan Democratic Party
1945	Azerbaijan Democratic Party announces formation of Azerbaijan Democratic Republic
1946	Red Army withdraws from Iran
1946	Azerbaijan Democratic Republic falls

1949	First publication in book form of Mirza Ibrahimov's The Coming Day
1951	The Coming Day receives Lenin Prize
1955	Presidium of USSR Academy of Sciences names Institute of Oriental Studies in Baku "a major center for Iranian studies in our country"
1955	Radio Baku begins broadcasts directed at Iranian Azerbaijan
1976	Section for "study and publication of Southern Azeri literature" formed under the Nizami Institute of Literature of the AzSSR Academy of Sciences
1978	Ouster of Shah
1979-1983	Iranian Azeri publishing activity revived in Iran
1979	Institutions concerned with "Southern question begin to multiply in the AzSSR
1979	Azeri literary delegation in England interviews Iranian Azeri students on their aspirations for the future of Iranian Azerbaijan
1981	Balash Azaroghlu, a 1946 emigre from the Azerbaijan Democratic Republic, named "peoples writer of Azerbaijan"
1982	Odlar Yurdu, a newspaper published for "compatriots abroad" by the Azerbaijan Society for Friendship and Cultural Relations with Foreign Countries, begins publication of an edition in the Arabic script for distribution in Iranian Azerbaijan
1982	"One Azerbaijan" slogan goes public in the AzSSR
1983	Tudeh banned in Iran; "progressive" Azeri publications closed down

Appendix B

Sheykh Mahammad Khiyabani (1880-1920)

Khiyabani was born near Tabriz, the son of a merchant. He attended a traditional Muslim school during his childhood and subsequently accompanied his uncle, also a merchant, on his travels in the southern Russian Empire; they resided in Daghestan for several years.

He returned to Tabriz for theological studies; in addition, he studied sociology, mathematics and history. His political involvement began during the Constitutional period in Tabriz, and he was a firm supporter of Sattarkhan's uprising. In 1909 he was a part of a delegation of landowners and members of the Democratic Party who were attending the 2nd Majlis (parliament) in Tehran. At that time, he belonged to no particular political party, but was leaning towards the liberal left. More importantly, he began to play a leading role in Iran's Jadidist movement, and formulated a political platform based on elements of a Muslim revival combined with liberal socialist doctrines.

In 1911 he journeyed once again through Russian Central Asia and the Caucasus, settling for short periods of time in Petrovsk, Vladikavkaz and Tiflis. Returning to Tabriz in 1916, he started the newspaper Tajaddod ("Renewal") in which he began to enunciate his Jadidist ideas. In 1918 he advocated an end to foreign intervention in Iran and reforms aimed at bettering the lot of small merchants, artisans, workers and farmers.

By 1920 Azerbaijani organizations of the
Democratic Party had grouped around him, supporting his position of "neither left nor right". In
the absence of any effective central authority
in Iran, he declared the founding of the republic
of "Azadistan" ("Land of the Free") in the Spring
of that year. "Azadistan" survived only some
three months. Khiyabani was executed when Iranian
troops reoccupied Tabriz in September 1920.

There are no studies in the West of either
Khiyabani or his movement despite the fact that
much of his political thought has been incorpor-
ated indirectly into the current social and political platform of the Islamic Republic of Iran.
It is worthy of note that at the height of his
prestige and authority, the Communist Party of
Iran was unable to penetrate or subvert his movement.

Mirza Kuchuk Khan (?-1921)

Almost nothing is known of Mirza Kuchuk
Khan's early life. He first came to the fore as
the leader of the Jangal guerrilla movement,
which was centered in the forests of Gilan.
Through his newspaper Jangal he advocated an end
to foreign interventionism in Iran, Muslim unity
and reforms aimed at bettering the lot of small
merchants, tradesmen and farmers.

In 1918 he turned, unsuccessfully, to the
Bolsheviks for support for his movement. In 1920,
however, he reached an agreement with them under
which he was to receive Bolshevik support for his
revolution. Under this same agreement, communist
propaganda was interdicted in Gilan due to the
religious fanaticism of the local population. Immediately thereafter, the founding of the Gilan
Soviet Republic with Kuchuk Khan at its helm was
declared. Within a short period of time, the Bolsheviks violated the terms of the agreement and
toppled Kuchuk Khan from power. He was replaced
by members of the Communist Party of Iran.

He and a companion froze to death in the
mountains in 1921 and a tribal chieftain subsequently delivered his head to Tehran. The
Jangalist movement itself fell victim to the
Soviet-Iranian Treaty of 1921.

Mirza Azhdaroghlu Ibrahimov (1911-)

Ibrahimov is the architect of the modern
phase of Iranian Azerbaijan's national liberation
movement. He was born near Sarab, a village in
Iranian Azerbaijan. In 1918 he emigrated to Baku
along with his father and brother. At the age of
eight, he was compelled to take a job as a labor-
er. After the full force of the revolution was
felt in Azerbaijan, he was educated at a factory
school and subsequently at the night school of
the Petroleum Technicum in Balakhany; during the
day he was employed as an apprentice metalworker.
He joined the Communist Party in 1929.

Ibrahimov started his literary career in
1930 with the publication of his first short
story. In 1932 he was elected a secretary in the
newly-formed Association of Azerbaijan Proletar-
ian Writers, the precursor to the present Azerbaijan Writers Union. He was then appointed to
the editorship of a newspaper in Nakhchyvan. At
the same time, he was able to continue his
education: he defended his Candidate's dissertation under Professor Bertels at the Institute of
Orientalism in Leningrad in 1936; his essay dealt
with the works of Mammadguluzade, the former
chief editor of the month journal of political
comment and satire Molla Nasraddin, which had
been the most influential opinion magazine in the
Turkic world from 1906-1932.

When the Red Army occupied northern Iran,
Ibrahimov was appointed editor of Vatan Yolunda.
In 1944 he was promoted to the post of Peoples
Commisar of Education of the Azerbaijan SSR. In
this capacity he toured Iranian Azerbaijan
shortly before the formation of the Azerbaijan
Democratic Republic. His novel, The Coming Day,
was conceived during his tours in Iran.

At war's end, he returned to civilian life
and combined his political and literary efforts
to work actively for the cause of Iranian Azerbaijan. To date, he has served several times as
chairman of the Azerbaijan Writers Union and has
been chairman of the Soviet Committee for Solidarity with the Countries of Asia and Africa
since 1977. Dating from the same period, he was
named director of the Section for Southern Azeri

Language and Literature at the Nizami Institute
of Literature.

Balash Abizade-Azaroghlu (1921-)

Born in Baku of Iranian Azeri parents, he
returned with his family to Iran in 1938. He
joined the Tudeh Party in 1942, and held various
positions in the government of the Azerbaijan
Democratic Republic in 1945-1946.

Azaroghlu emigrated to Soviet Azerbaijan in
1946 and established a career as a poet writing
about the oppression of Iranian Azeri national
aspirations by the Shah of Iran. Highly regarded
as a poet, he was named "peoples writer of
Azerbaijan" in 1981. Next to Mirza Ibrahimov, he
is the most important activist in matters per-
taining to the "Southern question" in the Soviet
Union today.

Bibliography

Newspapers

Adabiyyat va Injasanat(Baku), weekly newspaper of
    the Azerbaijan Writers Union.
Azarbayjan Muallimi(Baku), weekly newspaper of
    the Azerbaijan SSR Ministry of Education.
Kommunist(Baku), daily newspaper of the Communist
    Party of Azerbaijan.

Books, Monographs and Articles

Agabekov, Georges. OGPU. New York, 1931.
Akademiya Nauk AzSSR. Rastsvet nauki Sovetskogo
    Azerbaydzhana. Baku, 1980.
Akademiya Nauk SSSR, Institut Vostokovedeniya.
    Zarubezhnyy Vostok: Yazykovaya situatsiya i
    yazykovaya politika. Moscow, 1986.
Alekperov, A. K. "Problemy istorii Azerbay-
    dzhanskogo yazyka", Sovetskaya Tyurk-
    ologiya, 2/1984.
Aliyev, M. M. "Ba'zi Iran matbuat organlary
    sahifalarinda Azarbayjan khalgi va onun
    manshayi masalalari", Protiv burzhuaznykh
    fal'sifikatorov istorii i kul'tury
    Azerbaydzhana. Baku, 1978.
Arif, M.(ed.). Azarbayjan Sovet Adabiyyaty
    Tarikhi, 2v. Baku, 1967.
Artamonov, I. Istoriya Khazar. Leningrad 1962.

Arutyunyan, G. S. Iranskaya revolyutsiya 1905–
    1911 gg. i bol'sheviki Zakavkaz'ya. Yerevan,
    1956.
"Azarbayjan Demokratik Firgasi", Azarbayjan Sovet
    Ensiklopediyasy. Baku, 1976.
Azarbayjan Dovri Matbuaty (1920-1979-ji illar).
    Bibliografiya. Baku, 1979.
Azarbayjan Tarikhi, II. Baku, 1964.
"Azarbayjan Yazychylar va Shairlar Jamiyyat-
    inin ta'sisi ughrunda birinji ijlasda gedan
    muzakiralar", Azarbayjan, 1/1980.
Azaroghlu, B. "Hijranly gunlarim sirdashy",
    Azarbayjan, 7/1981.
"Babak harakati", Azarbayjan Sovet
    Ensiklopediyasy. Baku, 1976.
Basgoz, Ilhan, "Varlyg: A New Cultural Movement
    in Azerbaijan", Turkish Studies Association
    Bulletin. II/3, 1979.
Baskakov, N. A. Vvedeniye v izucheniye tyurkskikh
    yazykov, 2nd ed. Moscow, 1969.
Belova, N. K. "K voprosu o tak nazymayevoy
    sotsial-demokraticheskoy partii Irana",
    Voprosy istorii i literatury stran
    zarubezhnogo Vostoka. Moscow, 1960.
_____. "Ot otkhodnichestva iz severo-zapadnogo
    Irana v kontse XIX nachale XX veka", Voprosy
    istorii, 10/1956.
Bor'ba za pobedu sovetskoy vlasti v Azerbaydzhana
    1918-1920: Dokumenty i materialy. Baku,
    1967.
Bromley, Yu. V. "Natsional'nyye aspekty dukhovnoy
    zhizni cheloveka v istoricheskoy
    perspektive", Aktual'nyye problemy
    natsional'nogo i internatsional'nogo v
    dukhovnom mire sovetskogo cheloveka, vypusk
    1. Baku, 1983.
_____. Ocherki teorii etnosa. Moscow, 1983.
Bunyatov, Z. M. "Novoye issledovaniya po istorii
    Azerbaydzhanskogo gosudarstva Sadzhidov",
    AzSSR AN: Tarikh, Falsafa, Hugug seriyasy,
    3/1980.
Burtsev, M. I. "Boyevaya deyatel'nost'
    vostokovedov v politorganov sovetskikh voysk
    v Irane", Oruzhiyem slova. Moscow, 1985.
Chapkevich, Ye. I. Bol'sheviki i burzhuaznyye
    revolyutsii v Azii nachala XX v. Moscow,
    1985.

"Dovlat mamurlarynyn kandlarda yarandyglary
faja'i ifsha etmak ichin Azarbayjan Demokrat
Firgasi tarafyndan Azarbayjanda demokrat
dovlatlarinin diplomasi mamurlaryna va Iran
selahiyyatdar magamatyna achyg maktub",
Azarbayjan(a), I/3-4, October-November 1945.
Frye, Richard. Iran. New York, 1953.
Gadzhiyeva, N. Z. Tyurkoyazychnyye arealy
Kavkaza. Moscow, 1979.
Gukasyan, V. and Tagirzade, A. "Fal'sifikatsiya v
izyashchnoy oblozhke", Kommunist
Azerbaydzhana, 11/1984.
Guliyev, Rashid. "Bir roman barada ra'ylar",
Azarbayjan, 10/1981.
Heyat, Javad. "Regression of Azeri Language and
Literature under the Oppressive Period of
Pahlavi and Its Renaissance after the
Islamic Revolution", First International
Conference of Turkic Studies, Bloomington,
Indiana, May 19-22 1983.
Ibrahimov, Mirza (ed.) Azerbaijanian Poetry.
Moscow, 1969.
Ibrahimov, Mirza. "Dur, vagti-sahardir",
Azarbayjan, 2/1984.
_____. Galajak gun. Baku, 1979.
_____. "Janub sovgaty", Azarbayjan, 5/1981.
_____. "Janubda dirchalish", Azarbayjan, 1/1980.
_____. "Ujalyghyn hikmati", Azarbayjan, 5/1983.
Ilghar, Gasham. [Poem], Azarbayjan, 7/1981.
Irandust. "Voprosy Gilyanskoy revolyutsii",
Istorik-Marksist, V/1927.
Kafesoglu, Ibrahim. Harezmsahlar Devleti Tarihi
(485/617-1092/1229). Ankara, 1956.
Kaltakhchyan, S. T. Marksistko-Leninskaya teoriya
natsii i sovremennost'. Moscow, 1983.
Khandan, Ja'far. "Iran Azarbayjanynyn vatanperver
shairlari", Azarbayjan(a), 1, January 1946.
_____. "Mirza Ibrahimovun Janub movzulary",
Azarbayjan, 10/1981.
Khiyabani, Sheykh Mahammad. "Khiyabaninin
nitglarindan", Azarbayjan, 5/1983.
Kocharli, F. K. "Rastsvet dukhovnoy zhizni i
natsional'noy kul'tury Azerbaydzhanskogo
naroda", Razvitiye natsii i natsional'nykh
otnoshenii v usloviyakh razvitogo
sotsializma: Materialy vyezdnogo zasedaniya

112

Byuro Otdeleniya Filosofii i Prava AN SSSR.
Baku, 1983.

Komissarov, D. S. "Iran: vzglyad v trevozhnoye proshloye (iz vospominaniy vostokoveda)",
Oruzhiyem slova. Moscow, 1985.

Lomov, B. F. "Rol' psikhologicheskoy nauki v razvitom sotsialisticheskom obshchestva",
Razvitiye natsii...Baku, 1983.

Menges, K. H. The Turkic Languages and Peoples: An Introduction to Turkic Studies.
Wiesbaden, 1968.

Minorskiy, Vladimir. "Dvizheniye persidskikh rabochikh na promysly v Zakavkaz'ya",
Sbornik konsul'skikh doneseniy Ministerstva Inostrannykh Del, III. St. Petersburg, 1905.

Nissman, David. "Iran and Soviet Islam: The Azerbaijan and Turkmenistan SSRs", Central Asian Survey, II/4, 1983.

_____. "The Origin and Development of the Literature of 'Longing' in Azerbaijan",
Journal of Turkish Studies, VIII, 1984.

Rawasani, Schapour. Sowjetrepublik Gilan: Die sozialistische Bewegung in Iran seit Ende des 19. Jhdt bis 1922. Bonn, n.d.

Rustam, Suleyman. [Poem], Azarbayjan(a), 3(8), March 1946.

_____. [Poem], Azarbayjan, 4/1980.

Saba, Ali Akbar. "Gushgu balabam", Azarbayjan(a), 3(8), March 1946.

Sapozhnikov, B. G. "Gotovnost' sovetskikh vostokovednykh kadrov k zashchite Rodiny",
Oruzhiyem slova. Moscow, 1985.

"Sarhadsiz soz sarvatimiz", Azarbayjan, 5/1983.

Seidov, R. A. "O natsional'nom formirovanii Azerbaydzhantsev v Irane", Voprosy natsional'no-osvoboditel'nogo dvizheniya na Blizhnem i Srednem Vostoke. Baku, 1985.

Sharif, Aziz. "Atam va man", Azarbayjan, 7/1980.

Shukur, Muzaffar. "Eynally-Eynaly", Azarbayjan, 6/1984.

Swietochowski, Tadeusz. "The Himmat Party: Socialism and the National Question in Russian Azerbaijan 1904-1920", Cahiers du Monde Russe et Sovietique, xix, janv.-juin 1978.

Taghiyeva, Sh. A. "Muasir Iran burzhua tarikhshunaslyghyna Azarbayjan khalginin

etnik birliyinin inkar edilmasi haggynda",
Protiv burzhuaznykh fal'sifikatorov... Baku,
1978.

_____. "Sheykh Mokhammed Khiyabani i
natsional'noye dvizheniye v Iranskom
Azerbaydzhane v 1917-1920 gg.", Iran:
Istoriya i sovremennost'. Moscow, 1983.

USSR Report: Baku Journal on National Liberation
Literature from Iranian Azerbaijan. JPRS, 18
August 1980.

Vahabzade, Isfandiyar. "Mubariza illarinin
tarannumu (S. Rustam poemalary)",
Azarbayjan, 12/1983.

Valeh, Hasan. [Poem]. Azarbayjan, 9/1981.

Valiyev, Kamil. "Oz sozunun soraghynda",
Azarbayjan, 3/1983.

Volodarskiy, M. I. Sovety i ikh yuzhnyye sosedy
Iran i Afganistan [1917-1933]. London, 1985.

Wimbush, S. Enders. "Divided Azerbaijan: Nation
Building, Assimilation and Modernization
Between Three States", Soviet Asian Ethnic
Frontiers. New York, 1979.

Index

116

Azerbaijani language.
   See Azeri language
Azerbaijanis. See
   Azeri Turks
Azerbaijan Journalists
   Union, 72
Azerbaijan National
   Congress, 34
Azerbaijan Society for
   Friendship and
   Cultural Relations
   with Foreign
   Countries, 3, 42,
   72-73, 91
Azerbaijan SSR, 9, 10,
   42, 91, 96
   establishment, 17-18
   southern, 45-47
   See also Soviet
   Azerbaijan Republic
Azerbaijan SSR Academy
   of Sciences, 45,
   46, 71, 92
Azerbaijan SSR State
   Television and
   Radio Committee,
   47, 72
Azerbaijan Writers and
   Poets Association,
   58
Azerbaijan Writers
   Union, 42, 46-47,
   56, 61(n8),
   85(n34), 91
   progressive writers,
   57-58
   propaganda, 49, 55,
   71, 72
Azeri language, 9, 10,
   12, 18, 65, 92
   ban, 13, 28
   broadcasting, 71-72
   politics, 51, 52, 59
   protection, 4, 13
   publications, 47-48,
   70
Azeris. See Azeri

   Turks
Azeri Turks, 1, 2, 3,
   4, 7, 28
   nationality, 92-95
   origins, 8-9
   political agitation,
   31-32
   See also Azeri
   language; Culture;
   Soviet Azeris
Azeroghlu, Balash, 53, 54,
   77. See also Azarogh-
   lu, Balash Abizade-
AzSSR. See Azerbaijan
   SSR

Babeks, 68
Baku, 13, 14, 15-16,
   17, 19, 101
Billuri, Hokuma, 53
Bolshevism, 27, 106
   Azerbaijan, 19, 21
   in Iran, 5, 88-89
   organization, 15-17
Border agreements, 13,
   14. See also
   Cross-border
   relations

Capitalism, 14-15
Caspian Sea, 14
Centralist policy,
   28-29
Chief Political
   Administration for
   Political
   Propaganda of the
   Red Army (GUPP),
   29, 31, 34
Chief Political
   Administration of
   the Red Army (GPU),
   31
Coming Day, The, 37,
   103, 107
   effect, 42-44
Communist Party of

Azerbaijan, 72
Communist Party of Iran
   (CPI), 16, 20, 22,
   25(n30), 28, 101,
   102. See also
   Peoples Party of
   Iran
Communist Party of
   Russia, 17, 19
"Comrade," 50
Constitution, Islamic
   Republic of Iran,
   13
Council of Azerbaijan,
   52
Counterpropaganda,
   30-31
CPI. See Communist
   Party of Iran
Cross-border relations,
   1, 2, 5
Cultural revival,
   27-28, 32-33
Culture, 4
   influence, 95-96
   Iranian Azerbaijan,
   32-33, 41
   literature and, 36-37
   See also Cultural
   revival;
   Literature;
   Religion

Dada Gorgut (journal),
   72
Daghestan, 13
Derbent, 13
Dual fatherland, 54-55,
   73. See also "One
   Azerbaijan" slogan
Dumanly Tabriz, 44-45
Duzgun, Huseyn, 50-51,
   58

Education, 14-15, 27.
   See also Propaganda
Emigration, 14, 81-82

Azerbaijan SSR, 42,
   47, 73
   literature, 53-54
Enzeli, 19
Ethnic groups, 8-9.
   See also Azeri
   Turks
Ethnogenesis, 5
   Iranian perception,
   12-15
   Soviet perception,
   9-11
Ethnolinguistics, 8,
   93. See also
   Languages
Exiles, 81-82
"Eynally-Eynaly," 77

Fakhraddin, Mammadali,
   70
Foreign intervention,
   21
Foreign Relations
   Department (AzSSR),
   72

Galajak Gun. See
   Coming Day, The
Gasumov, Mehbaly, 31
Georgia, 13
Germany, 28-29, 30
Gilan, 14
Gilan Soviet Republic,
   5, 18, 19, 20, 22,
   25(n30), 106
Gokcha, 13
Government, 17-18, 20,
   34
   "Azadistan," 21-22
GPU. See Chief
   Political
   Administration of
   the Red Army
Great Britain, 17, 19,
   27
Gulgun, Madina, 42, 53
GUPP. See Chief

118